PUSH

⬅ PAPER ➡

PUSH

PAPER

30 Artists Explore the Boundaries of Paper Art

Curated by Jaime Zollars

LARK

An Imprint of Sterling Publishing Co., Inc.
New York

WWW.LARKCRAFTS.COM

EDITOR
KATHLEEN McCAFFERTY
CREATIVE DIRECTOR
CHRIS BRYANT
**ART DIRECTOR &
COVER DESIGNER**
TRAVIS MEDFORD

FRONT COVER
Jen Stark
Spectral Zenith, 2008

PAGE 2
Hunter Stabler
Cymatic Donut Lattice Interior 2, 2007

FACING PAGE
Michael Velliquette
Babooma, 2010

BACK COVER, TOP LEFT
Yulia Brodskaya
Firmenich, 2009

BACK COVER, TOP RIGHT
Jared Andrew Schorr
Hurry Up!, 2010

BACK COVER, MIDDLE LEFT
Jayme McGowan
Flight by Kite, 2008

BACK COVER, MIDDLE RIGHT
Helen Musselwhite
Summer Owl Tree, 2009

BACK COVER, BOTTOM LEFT
Matthew Sporzynski
Valentine Candy Heart, 2006

BACK COVER, BOTTOM RIGHT
Rob Ryan
Nobody Remembers, 2006

Library of Congress Cataloging-in-Publication Data

Push paper : 30 artists explore the boundaries of paper art. -- 1st ed.
    p. cm.
  Includes art by Matthew Sporzynski and others.
  ISBN 978-1-60059-788-6 (alk. paper)
  1. Paper work. I. Sporzynski, Matthew. II. Lark Crafts (Firm)
  TT870.P88 2011
  745.54--dc22

                                        2010051853
10 9 8 7 6 5 4 3 2 1

First Edition

Published by Lark Crafts
An Imprint of Sterling Publishing Co., Inc.
387 Park Avenue South, New York, NY 10016

Text © 2011, Lark Crafts, an Imprint of Sterling Publishing Co., Inc.
Photography © 2011, Lark Crafts, an Imprint of Sterling Publishing Co., Inc., unless otherwise specified

Distributed in Canada by Sterling Publishing,
c/o Canadian Manda Group, 165 Dufferin Street
Toronto, Ontario, Canada M6K 3H6

Distributed in the United Kingdom by GMC Distribution Services, Castle Place, 166 High Street, Lewes, East Sussex, England BN7 1XU

Distributed in Australia by Capricorn Link (Australia) Pty Ltd., P.O. Box 704, Windsor, NSW 2756 Australia

If you have questions or comments about this book, please contact:
Lark Crafts
67 Broadway
Asheville, NC 28801
828-253-0467

Manufactured in China

ISBN 13: 978-1-60059-788-6

For information about custom editions, special sales, premium and corporate purchases, please contact Sterling Special Sales Department at 800-805-5489 or specialsales@sterlingpub.com.

For information about desk and examination copies available to college and university professors, requests must be submitted to academic@larkbooks.com. Our complete policy can be found at www.larkcrafts.com.

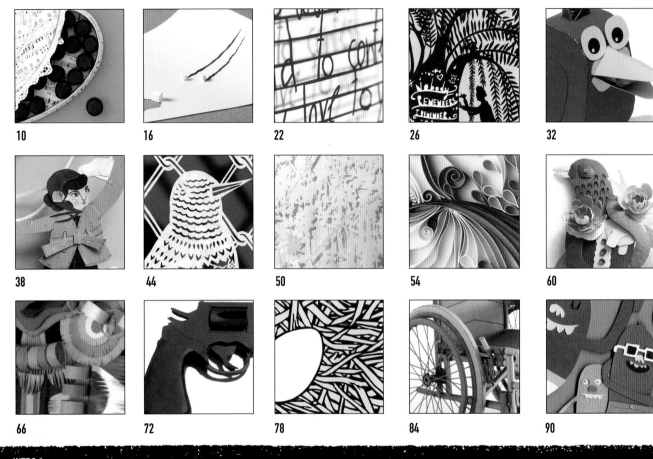

10

16

22

26

32

38

44

50

54

60

66

72

78

84

90

CONTENTS

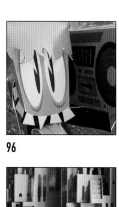 96

 100

 104

 110

 116

 122

 126

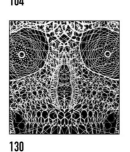 130

 136

 140

 144

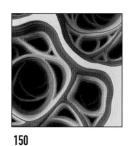 150

 154

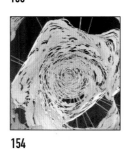 160

 166

Welcome to *PUSH*, an exciting new gallery series exploring contemporary artists who "push" the boundaries of traditional craft mediums. What does that mean in terms of paper? As it turns out, a lot. Within this book you'll discover paper architecture, engineering, sculpture, installations, and illustrations that will delight, amaze, and confound. You'll wonder: *How on earth did they do that?* Or perhaps, even: *Why?*

Though the art speaks volumes by itself, you can read insights from each of the 30 artists I interviewed, as they delve into their artistic impulses and examine why they do what they do. Think of *PUSH Paper* as your ticket into a private gallery with a chance to have an intimate one-on-one with the artist behind the work.

It's the unveiling of process, and the story of how, through curiosity, skill, and dogged determination, this material is not only transformed but re-imagined.

When I began my blog, Paper Forest, I set out to catalogue some of the astonishing paper art I was finding online at the time. It was unlike any work with paper that I'd ever seen before, with much of it coming from artists living overseas and in Japan. Over time, as the audience for paper arts grew, so, it seems, did the range of fine artists working with paper. In this international collection alone, you'll find artists with backgrounds in design, drawing, photography, sculpture, printmaking, Mathematics, performance, and more, with techniques born out

of cultural influences, repetition, experimentation, and a series of fortunate mistakes.

Collectively, these paper practitioners have educated grade-schoolers, launched community collaborations, and expanded on traditional techniques; individually, they have harnessed a sense of wonder and held fast to their instincts. As you will soon see, they challenge the boundaries of paper as a creative medium and transform a common material into extraordinary art. I hope you are as inspired as I am by these artists as they push forward and choose passion over convention, and possibility over limitation.

Jaime Zollars

"I am always surprised to hear what my clients imagine I can make for them."

◀ CANDY HEARTS
2005 | 36 x 48 inches (91.4 x 121.9 cm)
Paper; cut, sculpted
Photo by Monica Buck

 **PLEATED BLOUSE**
2007 | 36 x 48 inches (91.4 x 121.9 cm)
Paper, papier-mâché; cut, sculpted
Photo by Monica Buck

POPCORN
2005 | 36 x 48 inches (91.4 x 121.9 cm)
Paper, papier-mâché; cut, crumpled, sculpted
Photo by Monica Buck

DESCRIBE YOUR WORK. I am a designer and illustrator with a specialization in paper and cardboard. **EARLY INFLUENCES?** Origami books. Theatre. I also had a great kindergarten teacher. **HOW DID YOU END UP WORKING WITH PAPER?** I have always loved making things—the paper things just came out best. **WHAT RESPONSES DO YOU GET TO YOUR WORK?** I've been surprised at how well it's been received. I support myself doing paper-related projects. Sometimes I get nice messages from people saying they like my work—people I haven't even met. **HOW HAS YOUR TECHNIQUE DEVELOPED?** I haven't done a job yet where there wasn't some painful lesson learned. **WHAT INSPIRES YOU THESE DAYS?** Thrift stores

and sidewalk finds. **WALK ME THROUGH A DAY IN YOUR STUDIO.** Let's just say procrastination is my true calling. I make a great cappuccino, and I pamper my dogs. I run a lot of errands, make phone calls, and send e-mails. Lunch is my favorite meal. In between, I sketch and cobble things together. **OTHER ARTISTS THAT INSPIRE YOU?** Joseph Cornell and

NUTCRACKER
2005 | 36 x 48 inches (91.4 x 121.9 cm)
Paper; cut, sculpted
Photo by Monica Buck

FIREPLACE
2005 | 36 x 48 inches (91.4 x 121.9 cm)
Paper; cut, sculpted
Photo by Monica Buck
Art direction by Heath Brockwell

James Thurber. **WHAT DO YOU LOVE ABOUT WORKING WITH PAPER?** The way it transitions from two dimensions to three dimensions and back. It's also pretty easy to predict how a sheet of paper will behave, and what it can do.

ROAD TRIP CAR
2006 | 36 x 48 inches (91.4 x 121.9 cm)
Papier-mâché; sculpted
Photo by Monica Buck

PUMPKIN PIE
2007 | 36 x 48 inches (91.4 x 121.9 cm)
Paper; cut, sculpted
Photographer Monica Buck

VALENTINE CANDY HEART ▶
2006 | 36 x 48 inches (91.4 x 121.9 cm)
Paper; cut, sculpted
Photo by Monica Buck

"A4 paper is as close to nothing as it gets. This gives me more freedom as an artist to create meaningful stories out of it."

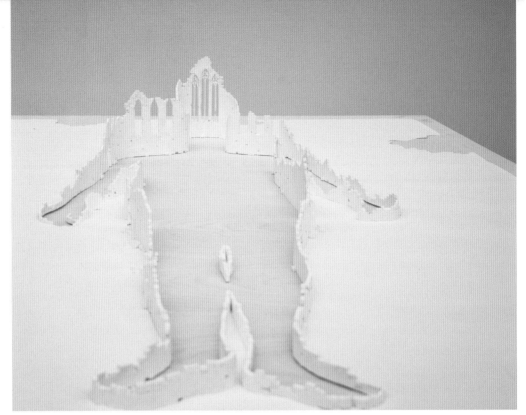

🏛 HUMAN RUIN
2008 | 101 x 57 x 10 inches (256.5 x 144.5 x 25 cm)
Acid-free paper, glue
Photos by Mette Bersang

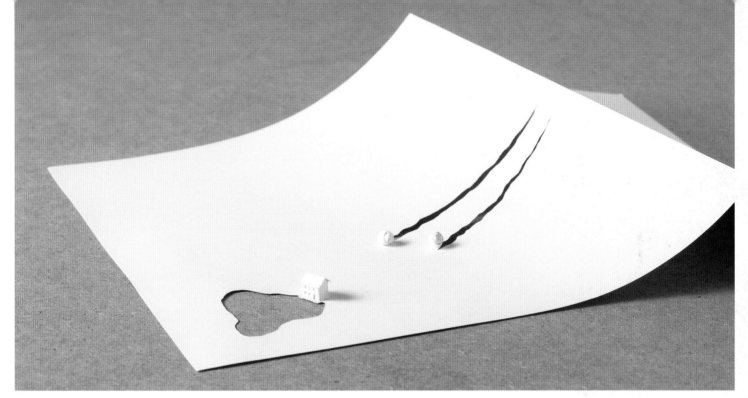

 **SNOWBALLS**
2005 | 8½ x 12 inches (21.6 x 30.5 cm)
Acid-free A4 paper, glue
Photo by artist

Q&A

DESCRIBE YOUR WORK. Lately I have worked almost exclusively with white paper to create different objects, paper cuts, installations, and performances. A large part of my work is made from A4 sheets of paper. It is probably the most common and consumed media used for carrying information today. **EARLY INFLUENCES?** I'm very inspired by Romantic painters and artists like Caspar David Friedrich, and Surrealist artists like René Magritte who contrast the magical and the impossible in their work. As my artworks are conceptual, I draw inspiration from artists like Piero Manzoni with his focus on the idea and the power of the mind. **HOW DID YOU END UP WORKING WITH PAPER?** It slowly developed from

IN THE SHADOW OF AN ORCHID
2005 | 8½ x 12 inches (21.6 x 30.5 cm)
Acid-free A4 paper, glue
Photo by Annabelle Dalby

performances where I was building things out of cardboard. These sculptures explore the probable and magical transformation of the flat sheet of paper into figures that expand into the space surrounding them. The negative, two-dimensional space left by the cut contrasts with the three-dimensional reality it creates even though the figures still stick to their origin without the possibility of escaping. In that sense, there is also an aspect of something tragic in many of the cuts. **WHAT RESPONSES DO YOU GET TO YOUR WORK?** People like the combination of the recognizable every-day material and the existential stories it tells. It's something that appeals to people of all ages. **WALK ME THROUGH A**

IMPENETRABLE CASTLE II
2005 | 8½ x 12 inches (21.6 x 30.5 cm)
Acid-free A4 paper, glue
Photos by Anders Sune Berg

DAY IN YOUR STUDIO. Coffee, e-mails, coffee, accounts, coffee, sketching, cutting, coffee, eating, sketching, cutting. **WHAT INSPIRES YOU THESE DAYS?** At the moment I'm inspired by words and language. Some of my new works deal with the question of whether language is able to mirror reality. **WHAT DO YOU LOVE ABOUT WORKING WITH PAPER?** By taking away all the information and starting from scratch using blank A4 paper, I feel I've found a material we can all relate to. At the same time, the A4 paper is neutral and open to different interpretations. The thin white paper gives the sculptures a frailty that underlines the tragic and romantic theme of my works.

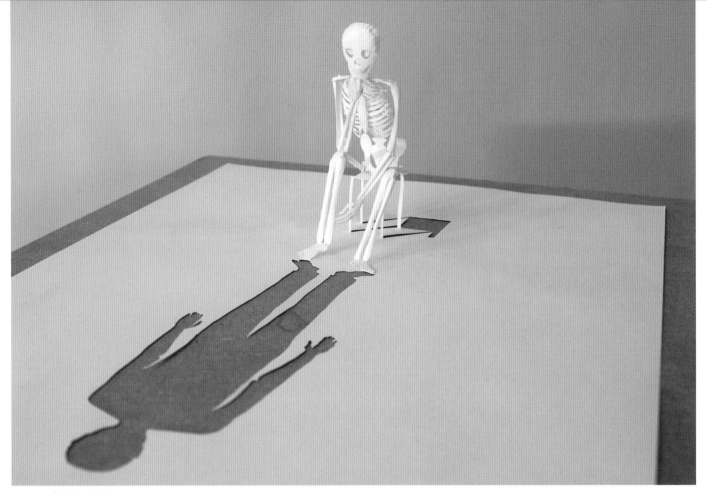

LOOKING BACK

2006 | 8½ x 12 inches (21.6 x 30.5 cm)
Acid-free A4 paper, glue
Photo by artist

DISTANT WISH

2006 | 8½ x 12 inches (21.6 x 30.5 cm)
Acid-free A4 paper, glue
Photo by artist

ANNIE VOUGHT

UNITED STATES

"With these pieces, my intent is to investigate the ghosts that we leave behind and to pay homage to those that haunt us."

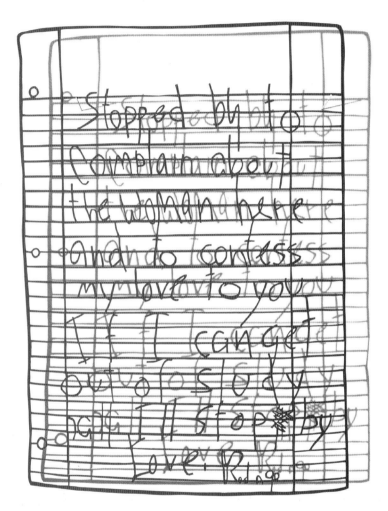

🔺 **GET OUT OF STUDY HALL**

2009 | 11 x 9 x inches (27.9 x 22.9 cm)
Paper; hand cut
Photos by Chris Fraser

◀ **DO I LOOK LIKE YOUR MOTHER**

2010 | 73 x 53 inches (185.4 x 134.6 cm)
Paper; hand cut
Photos by Chris Fraser

DESCRIBE YOUR WORK. I recreate notes and letters that I have found, written, or received by enlarging the documents onto a new piece of paper and dissecting the intricate negative spaces with an X-Acto knife. The handwriting and the lines support the structure of the cut paper, keeping it strong despite its apparent fragility. The sculptural quality of the letter allows the viewer to examine the care it took to render each piece in relationship to what is actually being said. The cutting is an elaborate investigation into the strange properties of writing. **EARLY INFLUENCES?** My parents strongly influenced my early work. They are both in the arts and taught me the value of creativity and believed in

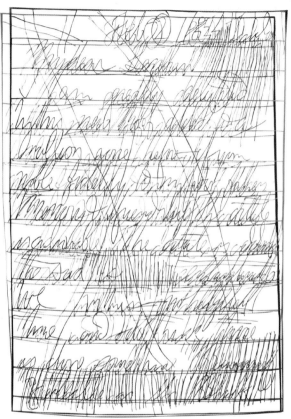

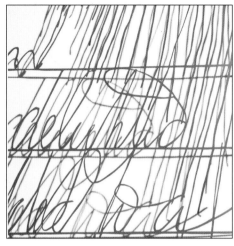

FEB. 2, 1854
2010 | 54 x 36 inches (137.2 x 91.4 cm)
Paper; hand cut
Photos by Chris Fraser

my intuition early on. **HOW HAS YOUR TECHNIQUE DEVELOPED?** A lifetime of practice and trial and error. I have made so many huge disasters. I have learned that the edge is cleaner on the opposite side of the paper that is being cut. So I cut everything backwards. I have also learned that even though my work on the whole is not very archival, I can do things to make it more so. Paper as a medium is temporary. **WALK ME THROUGH A DAY IN YOUR STUDIO.** My studio is in the back of a gym, so I have to walk through masses of sweaty people to get to the door of my studio. I share my studio with three wonderful artists; when I come in, someone is usually there. We talk for longer than is probably

I KNOW THAT THINGS WERE WEIRD BETWEEN US

2009 | 9 x 7 inches (22.8 x 17.7 cm)
Paper; hand cut
Photos by Chris Fraser

productive, and then I turn on an audiobook and get to work. I get so involved in my projects that I forget to eat. That's how things work when I'm in production on a project. On the other hand, I have a really hard time starting new projects, and I have a small crisis every time. I have a few friends I call on to go over ideas with me. My artistic group of friends is very important to me. **WHAT DO YOU LOVE ABOUT WORKING WITH PAPER?** For the time being I am communicating about correspondence and the written word. For me, paper is the perfect medium for that. I think that paper has an inherent beauty to it, and I believe that it is a very flexible and easy medium to work with

"We all really share the same one story; my work tells that story over and over."

NOBODY REMEMBERS

2006 | 31½ x 24¼ inches (80 x 62 cm)
Water-based ink, paper; hand-pulled screen print
Photo by artist

WE HAD NOTHING

WE HAD NOT MUCH

WE HAD ENOUGH

WE HAD EVERYTHING

◢ WE HAD EVERYTHING

2008 | 16½ x 18½ inches (42 x 47 cm)
Paper; hand cut
Photo by artist

EARLY INFLUENCES? The art that has influenced me the most is made by people who tell stories in their pictures. I loved Stanley Spencer when I was at college; he made me realize you could forge your own path and not be part of a "school" or "movement." I love Raphael, Titian, Uccello, Botticelli, Friedrich, Menzel, and Schinkel; Communist Chinese propaganda art, and USSR revolutionary ceramics. I love Bruegel—his pictures tell stories about people that are timeless. I'm also influenced by ancient Greek sculptures and their incredible ceramic decorations. **HOW DID YOU END UP WORKING WITH PAPER?** Coming from a printmaking background, I have always worked on paper. The way I

work is like stone carving: I end up with less than I started with. I was attracted to working in this way because of its austere simplicity—and it's fairly limiting, but within those boundaries you can be completely flamboyant and over the top, too. **HOW HAS YOUR TECHNIQUE DEVELOPED?** It's much finer and detailed than when I first started working on paper cutting. Essentially it hasn't changed too much because the thing that always drew me to it was its simplicity, and I

WE DONT FLY NORTH, WE DONT FLY SOUTH, WE STAY PUT RIGHT HERE YEAR IN-YEAR OUT! THE SEASONS CHANGE FASTER AND THE MONTHS GO BY QUICKER.
KEEP WATCH OVER YOU AND I KNOW THAT YOU'LL KEEP WATCH OVER ME

have found that trying to make it more sophisticated only detracts. Its strength is always in its plain directness. **HOW HAS YOUR SUBJECT MATTER EVOLVED?** I think that the evolution is so slow that I'm not really aware of these things as they happen. I tell the story of how I feel a lot, and I tell that same story over and over, albeit in many guises. **WHAT DO YOU LOVE ABOUT WORKING WITH PAPER?** I like it because you just need a knife, a pencil, a rubber, and a cutting mat to get

CAN WE? SHALL WE?
2009 | 51 x 37 inches (130 x 95 cm)
Paper; hand cut
Photo by Suzie Winsor

started on a picture. You don't need tubes of paint and brushes or water or turpentine. It is all very simple, yet very complicated—like me. **OTHER ARTISTS THAT INSPIRE YOU?** I am inspired by the American artist Maira Kalman. She is my hero. Anyone can paint or draw or make art, but to put into it kindness and decency and honesty is something that comes from the heart, and it shows. I also find the work of the English fashion photo by Tim Walker very inspiring

MY HEART
2010 | 51 x 37 inches (130 x 95 cm)
Paper; hand cut
Photo by Suzie Winsor

He has a joyful eye and when I look at his work, it always makes me want to create. He also makes me remember how beautiful the world is. The ceramic artist Grayson Perry is always challenging our preconceptions of how we see the world and how it really should be. He is a free and wonderful spirit and bright as a button.

ROB IVES
UNITED KINGDOM

"I really like the idea of bringing paper to life. Being able to use a simple mechanism to make interesting or unexpected movements is almost like magic."

SWAN
2009 | 7 x 7 x 3½ inches (18 x 18 x 9 cm)
230 micron matt board; inkjet printer
Photo by artist

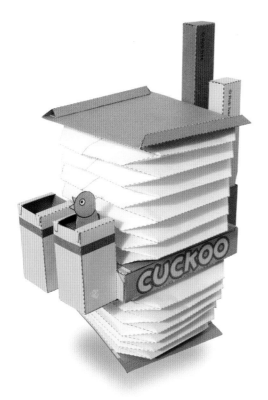

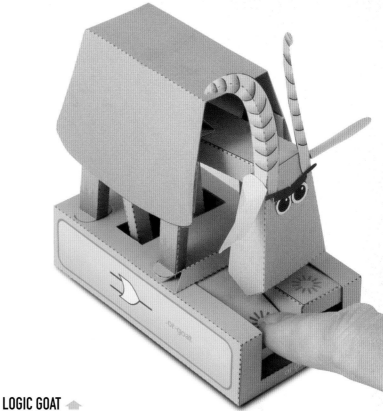

CUCKOO
2009 | 6¾ x 3¼ x 3½ inches (17 x 8 x 9 cm)
230 micron matt board; inkjet printer
Photo by artist

LOGIC GOAT
2009 | 3¼ x 2¾ x 4¾ inches (8 x 7 x 12 cm)
230 micron matt board; inkjet printer
Photo by artist

Q&A

HOW DID YOU GET YOUR START AS A PAPER ARTIST? I was a teacher for ten years and paper modeling was something I did in my spare time. One year, I made a model at a Maths conference and was approached by a publisher about writing and designing a book for them. The result was *The Paper Locksmith*, a collection of working locks to cut out and make. It sort of grew from there! **WHAT DO YOU LOVE ABOUT WORKING WITH PAPER?** I love the simplicity and immediacy. I love the way a couple of creases can transform a flexible strip of paper into a rigid strut. I like the bright colors, and I

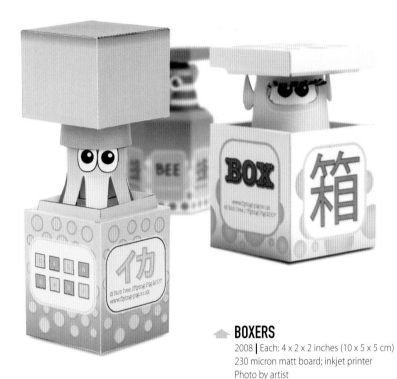

BOXERS
2008 | Each: 4 x 2 x 2 inches (10 x 5 x 5 cm)
230 micron matt board; inkjet printer
Photo by artist

TOO MUCH COFFEE
2009 | 6 x 3¼ x 3¼ inches (15 x 8 x 8 cm)
230 micron matt board; inkjet printer
Photo by artist

love the way that I can share my ideas with people all over the world. **EARLY INFLUENCES?** I used to see paper models designed by Peter Markey on family visits to Harrogate, North Yorkshire, when I was a teenager. I loved the way his simple automata designs brought paper to life. **OTHER ARTISTS THAT INSPIRE YOU?** I love the work of Paul Spooner, the

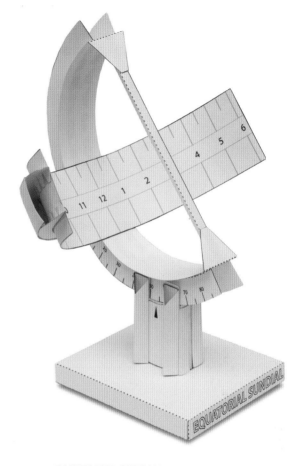

PAPER CROW
2010 | 4 x 2¼ x 2¾ inches (10 x 6 x 7 cm)
230 micron matt board; inkjet printer
Photo by artist

EQUATORIAL SUNDIAL
2010 | 4¾ x 4 x 4 inches (12 x 10 x 10 cm)
230 micron matt board; inkjet printer
Photo by artist

automata designer, and I really like Matt Hawkins for paper models. **HOW HAS YOUR SUBJECT MATTER EVOLVED?** Originally, I made automata models: paper animations with a box, a handle to turn, and a short story taking place on the top of the box—perhaps a sheep skiing, or a pig flying. Recently, I've turned more towards moving paper characters that

DOG ATE MY HOMEWORK
2009 | 4 x 2¾ x 4¾ inches (10 x 7 x 12 cm)
230 micron matt board; inkjet printer
Photo by artist

are free standing and self contained. **WHAT NEXT?** I have a list of unsolved mechanisms that I'd love to crack. Every so often I work one of them out, but a new one always comes along and takes its place. At the moment, I'm trying to make a model with a random element in it. What I want is a model where you pull a lever and your decision-making

GRRROBOT!
2010 | 6 x 4 x 2¾ inches (15 x 10 x 7 cm)
230 micron matt board; inkjet printer
Photo by artist

SNOWMAN
2009 | 4¾ x 3¼ x 3¼ inches (12 x 8 x 8 cm)
230 micron matt board; inkjet printer
Photo by artist

monkey raises a sign saying either yes or no, randomly. It's surprisingly hard to engineer randomness! **HOW HAS YOUR TECHNIQUE DEVELOPED?** I'm self-taught, so I pick up ideas and techniques wherever I can. Over the years, I've become more methodical in my working.

JAYME McGOWAN

UNITED STATES

"I like having to engage with a work of art by leaning in close, and feeling as if I'm peering into the window of another time and place."

FLIGHT BY KITE

2008 | 12 x 9 x 2 inches (31 x 23 x 5 cm)
Paper, glue, pencil, ink; hand cut and assembled
Photos by artist

AERIAL ADVENTURERS
2008 | 4 x 8¾ x 1 inches (10 x 22 x 3 cm)
Paper, glue, pencil, ink; hand cut and assembled
Photo by artist

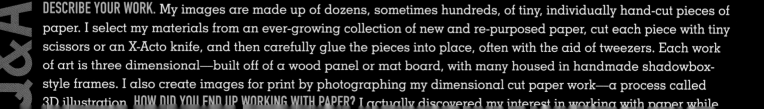

DESCRIBE YOUR WORK. My images are made up of dozens, sometimes hundreds, of tiny, individually hand-cut pieces of paper. I select my materials from an ever-growing collection of new and re-purposed paper, cut each piece with tiny scissors or an X-Acto knife, and then carefully glue the pieces into place, often with the aid of tweezers. Each work of art is three dimensional—built off of a wood panel or mat board, with many housed in handmade shadowbox-style frames. I also create images for print by photographing my dimensional cut paper work—a process called 3D illustration. **HOW DID YOU END UP WORKING WITH PAPER?** I actually discovered my interest in working with paper while

SECRET CONCERT

2008 | 4 x 8¾ x 1 inches (10 x 22 x 3 cm)
Paper, glue, pencil, ink; hand cut and assembled
Photo by artist

trying to quit smoking during college. I needed something to occupy my time and my hands, and was looking for a project where I could just sort of obsessively play with the materials. I turned to a pile of old thrift store books and began cutting. I found the construction method of cutting and gluing, cutting and gluing, over and over—requiring extended periods of focused concentration—to be pleasantly meditative and the humble materials of paper and glue to be surprisingly freeing. **WHAT RESPONSES DO YOU GET TO YOUR WORK?** Most people who see my work in person are shocked to see how tiny my pieces actually are, and wowed by the level of detail. "You must be incredibly patient," and "You should have been a surgeon, with such steady hands" are comments I hear a lot. For those that see my work in 2D as prints or on a computer monitor, usually the response is intrigue. The cast shadows from my pieces

being mounted dimensionally usually lead to a lot of questions about my process. I think people tend to be more interested in my technique above all else, but I do get nice feedback about the playful nature of my imagery as well. **HOW HAS YOUR TECHNIQUE DEVELOPED?** My work keeps getting smaller and more detailed. I'm almost embarrassed to say that I've considered working with a magnifying glass in my quest to place smaller and smaller details with tweezers. I've become a bit obsessed with trying to hide the supports that I make and conceal every last drop of glue. So my work has become even more labor intensive, but I think that it adds to the magic of a piece when viewers don't instantly know what they're looking at or how it was made. **WALK ME THROUGH A DAY IN YOUR STUDIO.** I like to start the day early. My studio is located in my home so I have to be disciplined, with a regular daily routine, if I'm going to stay

MAUDE ON A MISSION
2009 | 7 x 5 x 1 inches (18 x 13 x 3 cm)
Paper, glue, pencil, ink; hand cut and assembled
Photos by artist

EARL'S GOOD TUESDAY
2009 | 7 x 5 x 1 inches (18 x 13 x 3 cm)
Paper, glue, pencil, ink; hand cut and assembled
Photo by artist

focused. I also have music or public radio on in the background, always. I could honestly stay in my studio all day and never leave, so I have to force myself to go outside. I typically put in about 8 to 10 hours—sketching ideas for new pieces, sorting through paper, building frames, constructing the cut paper work, and photographing pieces, before I call it a day. **WHAT DO YOU LOVE ABOUT WORKING WITH PAPER?** What I love most is the finality of cutting and gluing a piece of paper. Not being able to erase or re-work mistakes like you might in a painting or drawing has been a really good thing. Destroy it and start over, or make do. It's great for a perfectionist like me who has a hard time calling a piece "done." **DO YOU DRAW YOUR IDEA FIRST, OR JUMP RIGHT TO THE CUTTING?** I do begin with a rough sketch, just to get the general composition down. The work changes so much when rendered dimensionally in cut paper, that I usually don't bother with precise and detailed drawings before

OUTLAWS IN THE ATTIC
2009 | 5 x 7 x 1 inches (13 x 18 x 3 cm)
Paper, glue, pencil, ink; hand cut and assembled
Photo by artist

beginning. As much as I like the work to take shape organically as the layers develop, I definitely try to make sure that I've got a solid plan before I begin. I often use my sketch as a size template for cutting some of the primary forms in a scene, just for the sake of saving time, and paper, with the usual trial and error. **FUTURE DREAM PROJECTS?** I recently had the opportunity to create artwork for a series of short animations and would love to explore that avenue further, particularly stop-motion animation. And I'd also like to make something that uses paper in ways I haven't tried before. Perhaps something the exact opposite of what I'm doing now, something very large—like a series of all-paper window displays or a theater set. I've also always wanted to collaborate with an author to illustrate a children's book and hope to be able to do that someday as well.

BOVEY LEE

CHINA

"I [ ] the sensation when the tip of the X-Acto knife touches the soft rice paper; the gratification it brings when a shape is cut out; the unstoppable, addictive nature of the craft; and the stillness."

ATOMIC JELLYFISH
2007 | 49 x 27½ inches (124.5 x 69.9 cm)
Rice paper; hand cut
Photos by Eddie Lam

LITTLE CRIMES I
2008 | 19 x 19 inches (48.3 x 48.6 cm)
Rice paper; hand cut
Photos by Eddie Lam

DESCRIBE YOUR WORK. I work with cut paper and create highly intricate and complex compositions within a single sheet of tissue-thin rice paper. Each impossibly thin strip of paper that I cut is integral in forming a broad narrative, a reservoir of visual and conceptual expressions that move between past, present, and future. **EARLY INFLUENCES?** My father, who introduced me to art, music, and books; my mother, who inspired many of my works; my grade school teacher, Mr. Ng, who taught me Chinese calligraphy when I was 10; and the Chinese folk artists of paper cutting. **WHY DO YOU WORK WITH RICE PAPER?** Rice paper in particular has both personal and cultural significance to me. It is the first art

◀ **RESCUE MISSION**
2009 | 23 x 22½ inches (58.4 x 57.2 cm)
Rice paper; hand cut
Photos by Eddie Lam

material I knew and used as a young student of Chinese calligraphy. The Chinese invented paper, and I feel a sense of intimacy and legitimacy in using it in my work. **WHEN DID YOU START CREATING YOUR PAPER CUTOUTS?** It began when I visited Hong Kong in the summer of 2004. My father gave me his small collection of paper cutouts, and I was immediately stunned with admiration. The urge to preserve, promote, and extend this fading art form ultimately

THE BUTTERFLY GOWN III ▶

2010 | 16¼ x 16¼ inches (41.3 x 41.3 cm)
Rice paper; hand cut
Photo by Eddie Lam

inspired me to develop paper cutouts as my own independent expression. **HOW HAS YOUR TECHNIQUE DEVELOPED?** I began my career as an artist at 10 when I practiced Chinese calligraphy. Over the years, I have pursued painting, drawing, printmaking, and digital arts. The technique I have developed for my paper cutouts involves hand drawing, digital rendering, and hand cutting. I begin by developing drawings then creating a digital template. The digital template

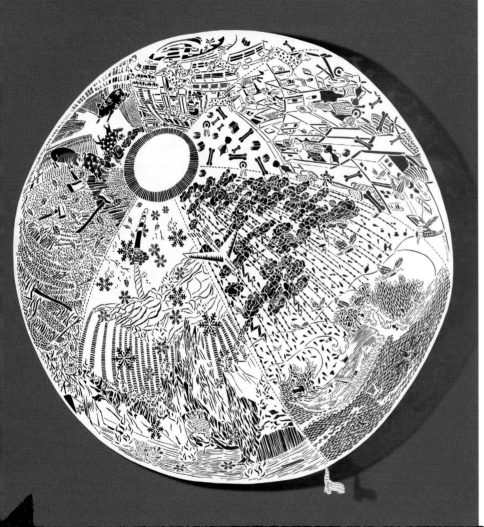

BEACH BALL BLAST
2009 | 20 x 18½ inches (50.8 x 47 cm)
Rice paper; hand cut
Photos by Eddie Lam

consists of downloaded images, my own digital photographs, scans from magazines and books, and vector graphics. The final step is for me to spend long hours, hand cutting the image with an X-Acto knife. **WHY DO YOU CHOOSE HAND CUTTING INSTEAD OF LASER?** I was told that even a laser couldn't cut some parts in my work because they are just too tiny. Regardless, I would

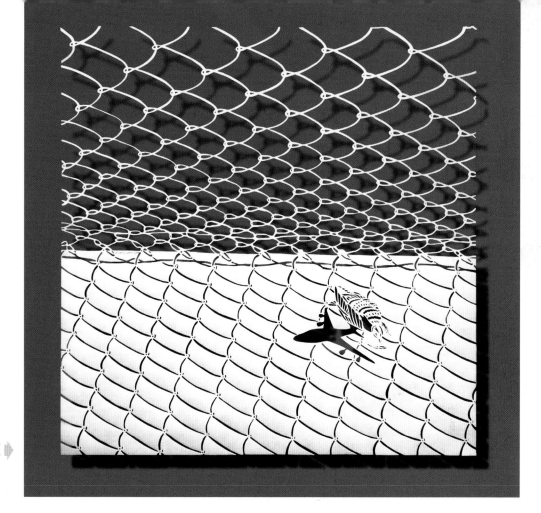

THE BIRD THAT THINKS IT'S A PLANE ▶
2010 | 12¼ x 12¼ inches (31 x 31 cm)
Rice paper; hand cut
Photo by artist

choose cutting by hand anyway—I like the subtle bodily movement, as well as the commitment, precision, and control it requires physically and mentally. It's very challenging but immensely gratifying. **WHAT INSPIRES YOU THESE DAYS?** Environmental issues, monarch-butterfly migration, and filtered/altered memory as an agent of comfort and survival.

"Cutting paper was a way for me to make landscape drawings that existed outside the traditional wall-hung rectangle, creating something that transcended two dimensions, actively encapsulating the viewer rather than passively hanging on the wall."

FERN SPACE BURST
2004 | Installation view, Headlands Center for the Arts, Sausalito, California
Variable dimensions
Hand-cut paper, colored ink, watercolor, iridescent medium, thread
Photo by artist

 **Q&A**

LANDING NOWHERE ELSE
2006 | Installation view, Bank, Los Angeles, California
Variable dimensions
Watercolor, iridescent medium, green tea,
tape, cut paper, thread, nylon netting
Photo by artist

DESCRIBE YOUR WORK. I make installations that transform interior spaces into site-specific environments. I begin by creating various sized paper-cut drawings in my studio. I then use those drawings as templates to fabricate new forms from different types of material. Those original paper cutouts and newly fabricated pieces are specifically hung and lit to create an immersive installation. **WHY DID YOU BEGIN TO CUT PAPER INSTEAD OF CONTINUE WITH TRADITIONAL DRAWING?** Just before I began cutting paper for the first time, I was making very large fantastical landscape drawings using charcoal and paper. These drawings tended to draw the viewer in through their dramatic use of perspective. At the

INTO THE SILVER SEE-THROUGH

2006 | Installation view, Bank, Los Angeles, California
360 x 228 inches (914.4 x 579.1 cm)
Tape, hand-cut paper, stainless steel nail supports
Photos by artist

WHITE WHITE MAYDAY IN MUSTARD AND GOLD

2006 | Installation view, Raid Projects, Los Angeles, California
Variable dimensions
Watercolor, white tape, cut white paper, thread, nylon netting
Photo by artist

time I had an uncontrollable urge to create extremely contrasting forms within the drawings. Unable to achieve this level of contrast using charcoal, I found a utility knife in my toolbox and began cutting apart the drawings. That was the "extreme contrast" I was looking for. Soon, I stopped using traditional drawing media and began using only a utility knife. **WHAT RESPONSES DO YOU GET TO YOUR WORK?** It is very important that the viewer is placed within the installation. I want the viewer to visually participate within the three-dimensionality of the artwork. In fact, I do not believe

an installation is complete until the viewer is drawn in and becomes implicated within its space. Since the viewer becomes a participant, I get responses typical from one going though an unexpected transformative experience.

WHAT DO YOU LOVE ABOUT WORKING WITH PAPER? Paper is the ultimate medium of economy. I am able to create expansive three-dimensional landscapes with a minimum of material. An entire, multi-faceted installation can be transported in a tube and "inflated" into a room-sized work of art. Plus, paper is the only medium that can easily be cut into

YULIA BRODSKAYA

RUSSIA

"I use paper strips in a free way to 'draw' with paper."

RAN OUT OF IDEAS
2008 | 16½ x 11¾ x ½ inches (42 x 30 x 1 cm)
Paper quilling
Photo by Michael Leznik

CITY ▶
2008 | 11¾ x 13¾ x ½ inches (30 x 35 x 1 cm)
Paper quilling; hand drawn
Photos by Michael Leznik

Photos by Michael Leznik

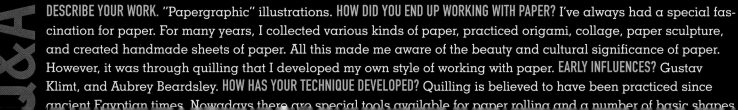

Q&A

DESCRIBE YOUR WORK. "Papergraphic" illustrations. **HOW DID YOU END UP WORKING WITH PAPER?** I've always had a special fascination for paper. For many years, I collected various kinds of paper, practiced origami, collage, paper sculpture, and created handmade sheets of paper. All this made me aware of the beauty and cultural significance of paper. However, it was through quilling that I developed my own style of working with paper. **EARLY INFLUENCES?** Gustav Klimt, and Aubrey Beardsley. **HOW HAS YOUR TECHNIQUE DEVELOPED?** Quilling is believed to have been practiced since ancient Egyptian times. Nowadays there are special tools available for paper rolling and a number of basic shapes

◗ RECYCLED CARD
2008 | 16½ x 11¾ x 1¼ cm (42 x 30 x 3 cm)
Brown card
Photos by Michael Leznik

to learn. However I never learned to roll those shapes, and I don't use any specially manufactured tools. I didn't even know that the technique was called "quilling" until my works became popular online. **WALK ME THROUGH A DAY IN YOUR STUDIO.** Answering e-mails; discussing projects or commissions with clients; cutting paper; making pencil sketches; transferring my pencil sketches to cardboard in order to glue the paper strips; shaping and gluing the

TWO FOR ONE
2008 | 11¾ x 11¾ x ½ inches (30 x 30 x 1 cm)
Paper strips
Photo by Michael Leznik

strips of paper (obviously this takes the most of the time); sometimes taking quick snapshots of the work in progress. **WHAT INSPIRES YOU THESE DAYS?** Good photography; creative typography. **OTHER ARTISTS THAT INSPIRE YOU?** Marian Bantjes, Si Scott, Jeff Nishinaka. **WHAT DO YOU LOVE ABOUT WORKING WITH PAPER?** The endless possibilities of what can be done with it, and the sensory feeling when you touch it.

FIRMENICH
2009 | 16½ x 23¾ x ½ inches (42 x 60 x 1 cm)
Paper quilling
Photo by Michael Leznik

PAPIER DE CREATION (ANTALIS)
2009 | 13¾ x 11¾ x ½ inches (35 x 30 x 1 cm)
Paper quilling
Photo by Michael Leznik

"I love paper, and I love the quiet process of working with this unique material."

◀ RED
2008 | 15 x 7 inches (38.1 x 17.8 cm)
Acid-free white and red paper, glue; hand cut, sculpted
Photo by artist

BIRD GIRL
2008 | 10 x 6 inches (25.4 x 17.8 cm)
Acid-free colored paper, glue;
hand cut, sculpted
Photo by artist

POR DENTRO
2010 | 13 x 6 inches (33 x 15.2 cm)
Acid-free ivory cotton paper, red paper, glue;
hand cut, sculpted
Photo by artist

DESCRIBE YOUR WORK. Most of the pieces that I create have a story behind them, related to myself or to someone else. Other times, I just want to create something for the sake of it. **EARLY INFLUENCES?** My teacher, Margarita, from the fourth grade. She would cut these interconnected paper flowers at the speed of light. I was really fascinated by how fast she was with scissors. I tried to do the same thing myself but my small hands and large scissors didn't get along at the time. **HOW DID YOU END UP WORKING WITH PAPER?** I first saw a few pictures of papercuts on the Internet and I asked myself: Who could imagine that you could do that with paper? My curiosity was so big that I couldn't stop thinking

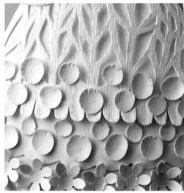

about trying something like that with my own hands. The rest of the story was ordering all the books that I could find on the subject of paper cutting, and learning the basic things that I needed to know as a beginner. **WHAT RESPONSES DO YOU GET TO YOUR WORK?** The feedback has been positive and thoughtful which I am extremely grateful for. When I hear and read what other people think about what I am creating, I feel inspired to keep developing my paper world. **HOW HAS YOUR TECHNIQUE DEVELOPED?** I can finally emulate Teacher Margarita with my scissors! The more I work with paper

◀ **HAND**
2008 | 9 x 6 inches (22.9 x 15.2 cm)
Acid-free white paper, glue; hand cut, sculpted
Photos by artist

the more I see all the possibilities of this amazing material. I'm looking forward to developing my technique even further. **HOW HAS YOUR SUBJECT MATTER EVOLVED?** As I grow personally, my subject matter evolves, because I get to experience life in a deeper way. In the end, my work is a reflection of my own vision, so I think that I'm growing along with my art. **WHAT INSPIRES YOU THESE DAYS?** My son, Diego, who is autistic and sees the world in such a unique way; my daughter, Natalie, who is an amazing artist; my husband, Bill, who teaches me so much with his quiet ways;

GROWING WOMAN
2008 | 11½ x 8 inches (29.2 x 20.3 inches)
Acid-free ivory cotton paper, glue; hand cut, sculpted
Photo by artist

my stepson, Miro, who is discovering life; and my mom, Margot, who had the hardest life ever but keeps her faith in other people intact. **WHAT DO YOU LOVE ABOUT WORKING WITH PAPER?** I will mention my three favorite elements: 1. It's a clean material, so you can work with it anywhere and clean up everything in seconds. For a busy mom like me, that's ideal. 2. When I make

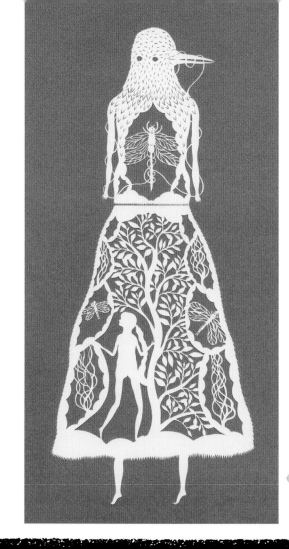

BROKEN HEART
2008 | 10 x 6 inches (25.4 x 15.2 cm)
Acid-free colored paper, glue; hand cut, sculpted
Photo by artist

LOST IN THE FOREST
2009 | 15 x 6 inches (38.1 x 15.2 cm)
Acid-free ivory cotton paper, glue; hand cut
Photo by artist

three-dimensional pieces with paper I get to explore the relationship between light and paper—they need each other, and I love that very much. 3. Paper is so versatile—you can cut it, fold it, draw on it, sew it, and more.

"I want my artworks to express abundance and exuberance, and for the viewer to experience an aesthetic of plentitude."

POWER TOWER
2009 | 108 x 72 x 25 inches (274 x 180 x 64 cm)
Cut paper, gator board, glue
Photos by artist

HONORED SOUL
2010 | 35 x 22 x 6 inches (81 x 56 x 15 cm)
Cut paper, gator board, glue
Photo by artist

HEART RAGE
2010 | 26 x 19 x 5 inches (66 x 48 x 13 cm)
Cut paper, gator board, glue
Photo by artist

DESCRIBE YOUR WORK. Early on I called my pieces collages, but as they got more textured and dimensional, I started calling them paper constructions. I think of them now as sculpture. They really need to be seen in person because there is this experience of the material that is very hard to translate in words, print, or digital imagery. **HOW DID YOU END UP WORKING WITH PAPER?** My very early work—mixed media sculpture—involved taking home craft or building materials and transforming them into spectacle objects and environments. Paper was always a material I used

PROPELLER
2010 | 14 x 15 x 2 inches (36 x 38 x 5 cm)
Cut paper, gator board, glue
Photos by artist

among others. Somewhere along the way I started making paper collage maquettes, and they ended up being the actual work. My art practice was at a place where it needed a kind of discipline, and working with paper allowed that to happen. **HOW HAS YOUR SUBJECT MATTER EVOLVED?** Several of my recent works have grown from a desire to create objects that express a devotional sensibility, and I have been looking at things like totems, stupas, altars, and

DIAMOND: RUMINATION
2009 | 14 x 14 x 6 inches (36 x 36 x 15 cm)
Cut paper, gator board, glue
Photo by artist

lingams. I have been doing some research on the early 20th century artist and occultist Austin Osman Spare. I became interested in a process he used to create symbolic forms called "sigils," and I've been working on a cut-paper series based on his process. **WHAT INSPIRES YOU THESE DAYS?** Perseverance, flamboyance, and a sense of the meticulous. **HOW HAS YOUR TECHNIQUE DEVELOPED?** As these works evolved, I began to look for ways to move beyond

the inherent flatness of paper to achieve the same sense of submersion that had been such an important part of my previous installation work. I spent time looking at other art forms like mosaic, relief sculpture, collage, and other paper-crafting traditions, and I have gone on to incorporate aspects of these forms into my work. The results have been ever-increasing levels of detail and dimensionality. OTHER ARTISTS THAT INSPIRE YOU? I still often look to Art Brut

BABOOMA
2010 | 32 x 32 x 9 inches (81 x 81 x 23 cm)
Cut paper, gator board, glue
Photo by artist

especially at the work of Adolf Wölfli and Augustin Lesage. There is a visual complexity and directness that I deeply appreciate. I've also recently been checking out several contemporary artists of Africa, and I think the Congolese artist Bodys Isek Kingelez is a visionary genius.

DANIEL SEAN MURPHY

UNITED STATES

"Paper is a very emotional and organic medium for me."

FLOWER STUDY ⬗
2010 | Life size
Paper, wire, glue
Photo by artist

GUN
2010 | 1 x 8 x 5½ inches (14 x 20.3 x 2.5 cm)
Paper, foam, glue
Photo by artist

DESCRIBE YOUR WORK. My work is made entirely from paper. I cut, bend, and glue papers together to replicate objects that are very familiar to me. I often create objects from memory or from a sketch of what I think something looked like. Occasionally, I use trompe l'oeil effects with paint to suggest shadow, depth, or age. **EARLY INFLUENCES?** In college I was inspired by Tom Friedman, Robert Gober, Charles LeDray, and Thomas Woodruff. I found that I could connect with their works and wanted to find my own unique voice along the way. **HOW DID YOU END UP WORKING WITH PAPER?** I was working on a large series of paintings for a group thesis show in college, when a professor suggested that I

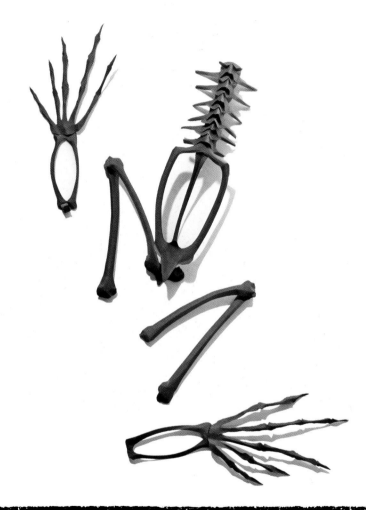

FROG ▶

transform some of the work into three-dimensional pieces. I created over 10 paper sculptures for the show and felt that I found a method of art making that worked for me. **HOW HAS YOUR TECHNIQUE DEVELOPED?** I think I've discovered ways to make paper transform visually to look like metal, stone, wood, or even something organic, like a leaf. In the past, I was dependent on paint to suggest a specific material; now I am able to do all of that simply with paper.

HOW HAS YOUR SUBJECT MATTER EVOLVED? I'm still focused on making iconic images, which are easily recognizable to

LUNCH
2009 | 9½ x 15½ x 1 inches (39.4 x 24.1 x 2.5 cm)
Paper, glue
Photo by artist

most people. I think what has evolved in my art making is how I approach each piece. When I first started making paper sculptures, I was obsessed with creating an illusion that the pieces were not paper and could be mistaken as real. Now, I'm almost doing the opposite—I'm letting the paper read as paper, while still giving the illusion of weight, age, and shadow. **WHAT DO YOU LOVE ABOUT WORKING WITH PAPER?** In some ways I feel like my whole life is wrapped up with paper. Sometimes, when I'm working on a new piece, I'll see a scrap, which reminds me of another

UNTITLED
2010 | Life size
Paper, foam, glue
Photo by artist

time, place, or piece. I feel a deep connection with this medium. **IS PHOTOGRAPHY IMPORTANT FOR YOUR WORK OR USED PURELY AS DOCUMENTATION?** I feel that my photographs are very important for my work; they help to build a mood—or evoke a

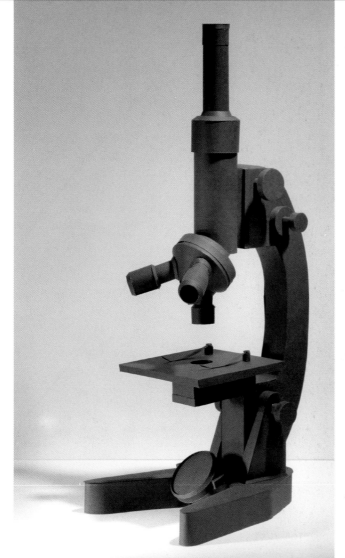

◀ **MICROSCOPE**
2009 | 16 x 5½ x 7 inches (40.6 x 14 x 17.8 cm)
Paper, foam, glue
Photo by artist

certain feeling with each piece. The black floral photographs were inspired by Baroque still-life paintings, and the microscope photograph was inspired by a science textbook from my childhood.

"I examine the positive aspects of being human: hands working, mending, making, people sharing, working collaboratively, imagining, and dreaming."

RELY

2009 | 11 x 11 inches (27.9 x 27.9 cm)
Paper; papercut
Photo by Dan Kvitka

 LEAR
2009 | 11 x 11 inches (27.9 x 27.9 cm)
Paper; papercut
Photo by Dan Kvitka

DESCRIBE YOUR WORK. My work is making papercuts. I focus on images from my life that connect to a collective memory. **HOW DID YOU END UP WORKING WITH PAPER?** I tried linocuts and scratchboard after a stint of technical scientific illustrations, but I wasn't happy with printing. It takes so long, even if it is magical. And I wasn't happy with the level of detail I could get with scratchboard—it was too much. I wanted to work with a knife so I couldn't erase; I couldn't be exacting. A friend who went to art school suggested I try cutting paper. I did, and a glorious feeling came over me. It's peaceful and meditative for me to work this way. **HOW HAS YOUR TECHNIQUE DEVELOPED?** I have been challenging

INVITE
2009 | 11 x 11 inches (27.9 x 27.9 cm)
Paper; papercut
Photos by Dan Kvitka

myself with shadows, distance, fingernails, faces, textures. My first papercuts are more cartoony. I use photos a lot now and stage shots with a digital camera. My work has become much more realistic, which is what I initially was trying to veer away from. **HOW HAS YOUR SUBJECT MATTER EVOLVED?** My subject matter has evolved with my life—which, thankfully has evolved! I am a wife and mother now. When I started I wasn't either of these things. My work records this transformation: the yearning and examination of the future. **WHAT DO YOU LOVE ABOUT WORKING WITH PAPER?** It is

◀ **EXTEND**
2009 | 11 x 11 inches (27.9 x 27.9 cm)
Paper; papercut
Photo by Dan Kvitka

delicate yet strong, and everything is connected, just like the larger world. **WHAT IF YOU MAKE A MISTAKE?** Some of my favorite pictures are ones where I made a mistake. I will keep cutting and am free to try new ideas out. Since I already
messed it up there is no fear of ruining it! Working with a knife allows me to be imperfect. **HOW LONG DOES IT TAKE YOU
TO MAKE A PICTURE?** I give myself a week. I'm too impatient to go beyond that and lose my curiosity, too. Plus, I tend to
schedule down to the last minute and it *has* to be done in a week. **WHAT INSPIRES YOU THESE DAYS?** My family, hands,

RESUME

©Nikki McClure

RESUME
2008 | 11 x 11 inches (27.9 x 27.9 cm)
Paper; papercut
Photo by Dan Kvitka

(always hands at work), touching, eye contact, moss, tall grasses, ancient and gnarled trees. Foraging always lifts my spir-its. So does cooking when the whole oven is filled. Also: eggs, builders, farmers, mushrooms, and symbiosis. **OTHER ARTISTS**

RETURN

RETURN
2005 | 11 x 11 inches (27.9 x 27.9 cm)
Paper; papercut
Photo by Michael Ryan

THAT INSPIRE YOU? Mecca Normal, Calvin Johnson, Maurice Sendak, Robert McCloskey, Tove Jansson, Swoon, Miriam Klein Stahl, Kathe Kollwitz, Winslow Homer, Frans Masereel, and Mary Cassatt.

CHRIS GILMOUR

UNITED KINGDOM

"One of the reasons I am attracted to cardboard is its resonance as a material and its ubiquity—almost as if it were a natural material like wood or stone."

⌂ WHEELCHAIR

2003 | Life size
Cardboard, glue
Photo by Marco De Palma

THE TRIUMPH OF GOOD AND EVIL
2009 | 71 x 83 x 31½ inches (180 x 210 x 80 cm)
Cardboard, glue
Photo by Marco De Palma

Q&A

DESCRIBE YOUR WORK. I make hyper-realistic sculpture using cardboard boxes. The work is all handmade using only glue and cardboard—there is no supporting structure of wood or metal. The finished works create an effect where the viewer tries to reconcile the solid physical presence of well-known objects with a material which most people think of as light, weak, and only meant to be thrown away. The work can be seen as a reflection on consumerism and materialism, and as metaphor for transience and impermanence, but it is played out through the spirit of an

FIAT 500

2001 | Life size
Cardboard, glue
Photo by Marco De Palma

object and the associations it calls up, which makes it very immediate and attractive. **HOW DID YOU END UP WORKING WITH PAPER?** I've always preferred sculpture. I studied stone carving, metal work, and bronze casting, but I found myself becoming more and more fascinated by cardboard and paper. The work with cardboard is a series of techniques I have invented over the years and the fruit of a lot of experimentation. It's not really a technique they teach you at art school. **WHAT RESPONSES DO YOU GET TO YOUR WORK?** People always want to touch it. I think the best example of this was

QUEEN VICTORIA ▶
2008 | Life size
Cardboard, glue
Photo by Marco De Palma

with a wheelchair that was in a show in Milan. One elderly gentleman was so taken with the work that he couldn't resist trying it—of course the moment he sat on it, and it broke to pieces, the illusion was shattered. It was the end of that piece, but it's nice to get people so enchanted with the work. **HOW HAS YOUR TECHNIQUE DEVELOPED?** I studied sculpture at university, so I have a background in traditional sculpture techniques, but my artwork is based on a series of techniques I've developed over the years. Mostly, the cardboard is just cut and folded. A lot of the work

lies in thinking of how to make the sculptures, and how to make sure they will survive over time. It took me nearly three years to find a way to make the bikes stand up. Recent work is based on classical statues and making these is more fluid. **HOW HAS YOUR SUBJECT MATTER EVOLVED?** The choice of everyday objects calls up memories and emotions connected to our experience of these things. Since my approach is both visual and conceptual, I choose objects for their visual appeal and cultural resonance, and I also choose objects that imply an action or interaction of some sort.

3 BIKES

2003 | Life size
Cardboard, glue
Photo by Marco De Palma

WHAT DO YOU LOVE ABOUT WORKING WITH PAPER? I like the illusion of reality that is created by my sculptures. They are like the ghosts of objects, and they bring the viewer into a relationship with the object that, ultimately, is not real. I think this creates a kind of short circuit in the viewer. People want to use the objects, but of course they can't.

JARED ANDREW SCHORR

UNITED STATES

"I'm still, and will probably always be, expanding my visual vocabulary."

HIDE AND SEEK

2010 | 20 x 20 x 2 inches (50.8 x 50.8 x 5.1 cm)
Paper, foam tape, glue; papercut
Photo by artist

DO GOOD
2010 | 7 x 11 inches (17.8 x 27.9 cm)
Paper, foam tape, glue; papercut
Photo by artist

DESCRIBE YOUR WORK. I try to make pictures that make people happy. **HOW DID YOU END UP WORKING WITH PAPER?** I ended up working with paper in school. Everyone was drawing with ink and watercolor, and I wanted to venture out, try to carve my own path. I loved photo collage, but I didn't want to deal with copyright issues so I just started using flat cardstock. **WHAT RESPONSES DO YOU GET TO YOUR WORK?** I get a lot of pitchforks and torches. I'm fine with pitchforks. American Gothic is fun to reenact with the wife. But torches around paper, COME ON! **HOW HAS YOUR TECHNIQUE DEVELOPED?** My technique changes with each piece. It's what makes cutting paper exciting to me. Each piece is

HURRY UP!
2010 | 6 x 12 x 1 inches (15.2 x 30.5 x 2.5 cm)
Paper, foam tape, glue; papercut
Photo by artist

a new learning experience. I've also noticed that as time goes on, pieces get more complex, and it's extremely satis-fying to see all those parts come together. **WALK ME THROUGH A DAY IN YOUR STUDIO.** I take my son to daycare. I come home and eat as I check my e-mail. Then I'll draw for like 45 minutes regardless of what's on the agenda for the day. I guess this is equivalent to an athlete stretching; just shaking off the cobwebs. Then I'll cut until about 5 pm, usually

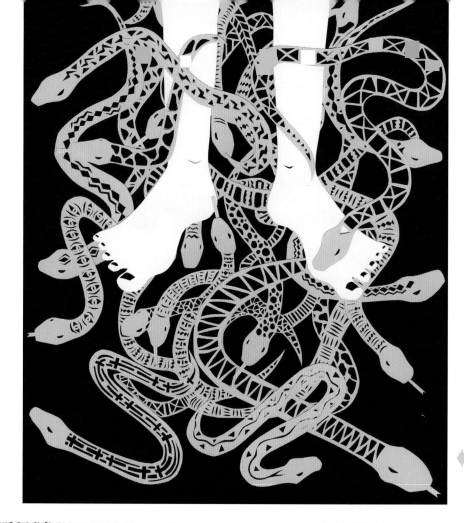

◀ **HOLY RATTLESNAKES**
2009 | 16 x 20 x 1 inches (40.6 x 50.8 x 2.5 cm)
Paper, foam tape, glue; papercut
Photo by artist

trying to make deadlines. Then I hang out with my family until they go to bed at around 9:30 pm. I usually cut or draw until 12:30 am. I try to work 8 to 10 hours a day. **HOW HAS YOUR SUBJECT MATTER EVOLVED?** I'm always finding different ways to develop subject matter. It's important to keep yourself on your toes. If you don't, then things get stale, so you learn and grow. **WHAT INSPIRES YOU THESE DAYS?** Having my wife and kids is truly inspiring. I just want to make

BLESS THIS HUT
2010 | 10 x 8 x 1½ inches (25.4 x 20.3 x 3.8 cm)
Paper, foam tape, glue; papercut
Photo by artist

things that make them happy and smile. There's nothing better. **OTHER ARTISTS THAT INSPIRE YOU?** Ralph Steadman, Ray Johnson, Herge, Charles Shulz, Steve Martin, Jim Houser, Souther Salazar, S. Britt, and Richard Scarry. **WHAT DO YOU LOVE ABOUT WORKING WITH PAPER?** This sounds weird, but I love the fact that paper is physical. I still have to use my hands to manipulate i

MONSTER ALPHABET

2010 | 11 x 8½ inches (27.9 x 21.6 cm)
Paper, foam tape, glue; papercut
Photo by artist

In that way it is like painting. The end result is something that I can hold in my hands. I see my own work, and I am still kind of amazed that I am the one who created it. WHAT PIECE OF ART WOULD YOU MOST LIKE TO SEE IN PERSON? Marcel Duchamp's *Tu m'*

OLIVER OLLIE

2008 | 5 x 4 x 2 inches (12.7 x 10.2 x 5.1 cm)
Paper, digital print
Photo by artist

PAPER PAC
2009 | 10 x 14 x 7 inches (25.4 x 35.6 x 17.8 cm)
Colored paper
Photo by artist

Q&A

DESCRIBE YOUR WORK. Dimensional paper art toys with personality, life, action, and humor. **EARLY INFLUENCES?** I spent most of my childhood drawing my favorite cartoons from old animation and comic strips. I loved the classic *Looney Tunes* and *The Muppet Show*. I filled many notebooks with scratchy drawings of Bugs Bunny and Daffy Duck; pages that should have been filled with history notes and math equations. I used to check out old books from the library and practice drawing characters like Walt Kelly's *Pogo*, and Floyd Gottfredson's Mickey Mouse. I was also a big fan of John Kricfalusi's *Ren & Stimpy*. **HOW DID YOU END UP WORKING WITH PAPER?** I was working at a large Midwest greeting

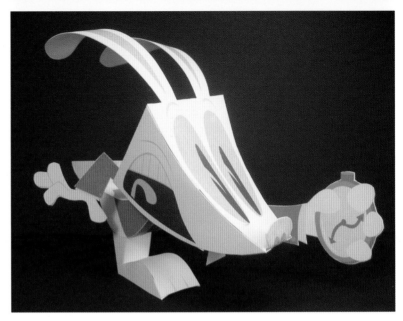

card company as a production artist, and one day out of boredom I turned over a disposable cup, drew a face on it, and cut hands and feet out of index cards. Then I started making more elaborate cup and index card creations, veering towards dimensional paper sculpture. Around this same time I came across the Paper Forest blog and was instantly fascinated by all the cool papercraft and paper toys to be found online. I decided to do a paper toy of a character from a comic book I just finished and was instantly hooked! **WHAT RESPONSES DO YOU GET TO YOUR WORK?** It's interesting to watch people's reaction to my work, especially in a gallery setting. Some dismiss it pretty quickly based on the obvious humor and cartoon-type quality, but overall, I think most people are drawn in by the fun and

colorful characters, and then they notice the paper engineering and are pretty impressed by the technical skill it takes to conceive this stuff. People seem to respond pretty strongly one way or the other. I also get e-mails from all over the world with awesome photos from people who have downloaded and built my paper toys. **WHAT INSPIRES YOU THESE DAYS?** I'm super-inspired by my kids. Viewing the world through their eyes really helps me see the world anew with wonder and optimism. Their enthusiasm, energy, love, and laughter is infectious and inspiring. I also have a passion for music. If I'm not drawing, cutting, or folding, I'm usually playing music, and that's reflected in a lot of my work. **WHAT DO YOU LOVE ABOUT WORKING WITH PAPER?** It's humble, widely available, and super versatile.

UNTITLED (YELLOW BOOK)
2008 | 9½ x 17 x 2 inches (5.1 X 43.2 X 24.1 x 43.2 x 5.1 cm)
Ledger paper, drafting knife; hand cut, glued
Photos by artist

"With each piece, the notion of 'value' is called into question—be it the value of our quotidian pursuits, the relative value of labor, or the implicit values of economic advancement."

UNTITLED (RECONSTRUCTION 4)
2009 | 6½ x 6½ inches (16.5 x 16.5 cm)
Ledger paper, matte board; drafting knife,
hand cut, glued
Photo by artist

DESCRIBE YOUR WORK. Ledger sheets are traditionally used to record the financial transactions of a business or an individual, and for analysis in determining profit and loss. They are the material of economics. In an attempt to understand our need to quantify our transactions, I employ this paper. I use a drafting knife to individually remove tens of thousands of boxes, leaving behind the lattice of the grid intended to separate the boxes. I involve myself in this routine of trying to make time and labor palpable while communicating its loss. The skeletal pages drape

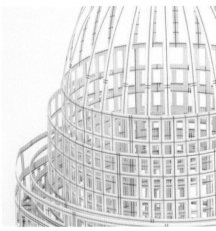

and accumulate, demarcate the time cost for their creation, and become the buildings for which they have laid the groundwork. Grids are reconstructed using the excised boxes in order to create a new sense, a new value. The boxes become the units of the picture plane, the medium of color fields. **EARLY INFLUENCES?** My background is in printmaking, so that process, specifically the repetitive nature of that process, has always been influential. **HOW DID YOU END UP WORKING WITH PAPER?** It started out as an exploration of the meaning and value of "work," or "labor." I was interested in the differences between my work as an artist and the work (perhaps more practical work) of other people in my

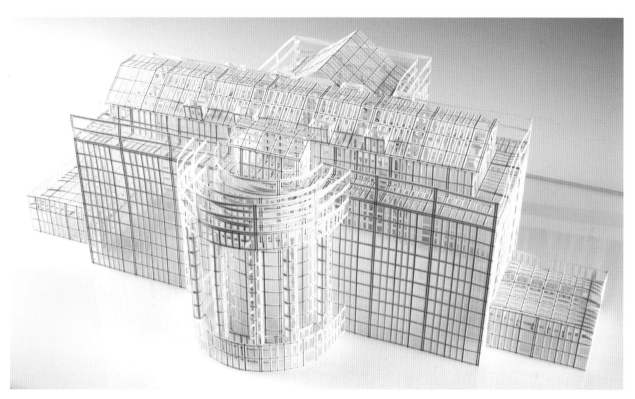

UNTITLED (WHITE HOUSE)

2007 | 4 x 11 x 6½ inches (10.2 x 27.9 x 16.5 cm)
Ledger paper, drafting knife; hand cut, glued
Photo by artist

family. I eventually took up my father's ledger paper. Before I was old enough to understand what this paper was actually for, I knew it as my dad's "work paper." I've been working exclusively with ledger paper since then. **HOW HAS YOUR SUBJECT MATTER EVOLVED?** I think that the subject matter evolved from something very personal to something that is universal, or perhaps it's been both all along. **OTHER ARTISTS THAT INSPIRE YOU?** My all-time favorites are Agnes Martin, Hanne Darboven, Ann Hamilton, and Robert Ryman.

JEN STARK
UNITED STATES

"I try to make static lines and colors move, and make the viewer's eyes vibrate."

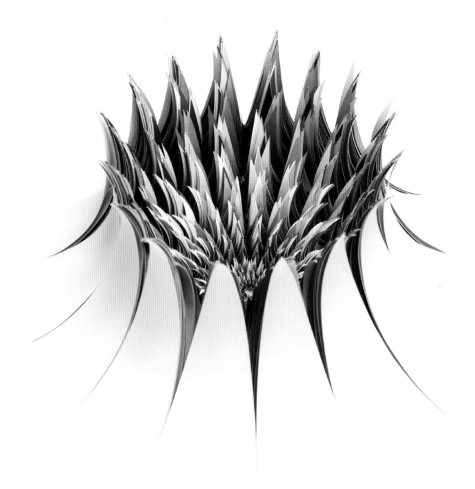

BURST
2007 | 12 x 12 x 3 inches (30.5 x 30.5 x 7.6 cm)
Acid-free paper
Photo by Harlan Erskine

SPECTRAL ZENITH
2008 | 20 x 20 x 4 inches (50.8 x 50.8 x 10.2 cm)
Acid-free paper on wood.
Photo by artist

DESCRIBE YOUR WORK. I create mathematically organic, colorful, and intricate paper sculptures. My work is inspired by all sorts of things, from wormholes, to how micro and macro designs relate to each other, to the layers of plants. **EARLY INFLUENCES?** Tom Friedman and Andy Goldsworthy were a couple of my artistic influences early on. Also, my grandfather was a big influence on me becoming an artist. He was a hobby watercolor painter and would invite me over to have art lessons with him. **HOW DID YOU END UP WORKING WITH PAPER?** It started when I went to study abroad in France. I was only allowed two suitcases on the plane, so I decided to purchase art supplies when I got there. The

euro was very high and things were expensive, so when I went into the art store I looked around for a cheap material, but one that had potential. I walked out with a stack of colored construction paper and began experimenting, and it took off from there. **WHAT RESPONSES DO YOU GET TO YOUR WORK?** Most people get inspired by it, which is great! I think that's the best an artist can ask for. Also, I think it is interesting how many different kinds of people from all walks of life seem to enjoy my work. I'd love to inspire as many people as possible. **HOW HAS YOUR TECHNIQUE DEVELOPED?** My technique has developed because of all the practice I've had. I've gotten better at making more precise cuts with my X-Acto

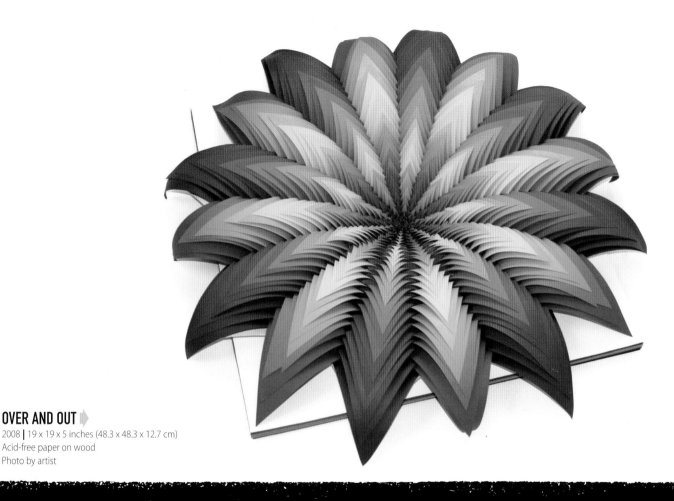

OVER AND OUT ⏩
2008 | 19 x 19 x 5 inches (48.3 x 48.3 x 12.7 cm)
Acid-free paper on wood
Photo by artist

WALK ME THROUGH A DAY IN YOUR STUDIO. I wake up (late morning), have some breakfast, then start working. I usually listen to NPR and have a large table to work on. I always have a big cutting board under what I'm working on and have stacks of paper ready to be cut. I go through about an X-Acto a day, sometimes more. **WHAT INSPIRES YOU THESE DAYS?** I'm inspired by all sorts of things, from outer space, to underwater creatures and plants, to microscopic designs in nature and evolution. **WHAT DO YOU LOVE ABOUT WORKING WITH PAPER?** I love how paper is such a common material and is used in everyday life. I think it is overlooked and has so much potential. I also love the idea of turning something 2D into 3D

PIECE OF AN INFINITE WHOLE

2008 | 24 x 24 x 48 inches (61 x 61 x 122 cm)
Acid-free paper, light
Photo by Harlan Erskine

CORIOLIS EFFECT

2007 | 12 x 12 x 3 inches (30.5 x 30.5 x 7.6 cm)
Acid-free paper on wood
Photo by Harlan Erskine

KEISUKE SAKA

JAPAN

"Creating things with our hands, just by cutting, folding, and pasting will remind people—even grown-ups—of a simple delight and surprise. And we don't have to worry if we fail. It's only paper."

110

◀ TEETER TOTTER
2001 | 10 x 5½ x 4½ inches (25.5 x 14 x 11.5 cm)
A4 paper; template
Photo by Natsuyuki Kishimoto

READY TO FLY (CLIMATE CHANGE)
2000 | 9 x 5½ x 5 inches (23 x 14 x 12.5 cm)
A4 paper; template
Photo by Natsuyuki Kishimoto

HESITATION
2001 | 9½ x 8½ x 7½ inches (24 x 21.5 x 18.5 cm)
A4 paper; template
Photo by Natsuyuki Kishimoto

DESCRIBE YOUR WORK. I design templates for papercraft models that people may assemble for themselves. My subject matter varies, but I am especially interested in automata models that are called *karakuri* in Japanese. **EARLY INFLUENCES?** When I was nine, I drew up a plan for a moving wooden toy. Later, my interest moved to manga, and I aimed to be a comic artist or illustrator in my teens. It was after becoming a graphic designer in my mid-twenties when my interest returned to three-dimensional forms. **HOW DID YOU END UP WORKING WITH PAPER?** The greater part of graphic design was owed to handwork with a craft knife and tweezers before the introduction of the computer, and

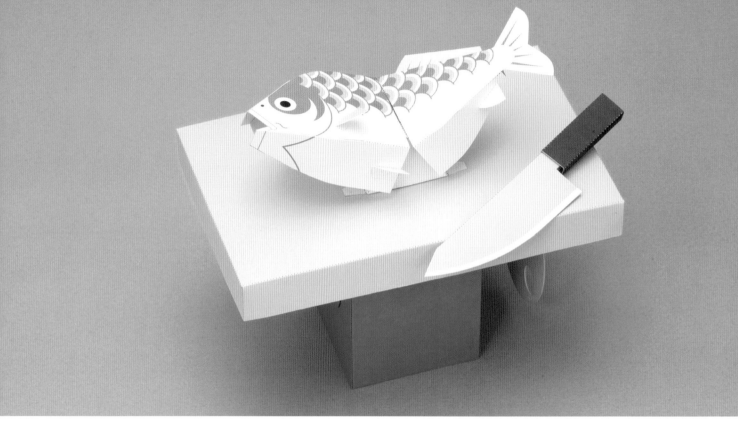

DOOMED

2002 | 5½ x 7½ x 5 inches (14.5 x 19 x 12.5 cm)

A4 paper; template

Photo by Natsuyuki Kishimoto

I loved it. I started to make pop up cards and paper models because it was the most familiar and cheap material for a young graphic designer. Around 2000, I had a chance to show my work in Denmark and Tokyo. After that I got commissions to make models. **WHAT RESPONSES DO YOU GET TO YOUR WORK?** The most delightful comments I get are from people who enjoy making and playing with my works with their family and friends. I often see a parent, who just

🔺 **MATERNAL DILEMMA**
2002 | 7¼ x 5 x 6 inches (18 x 12.5 x 15.5 cm)
A4 paper; template
Photo by Natsuyuki Kishimoto

🔺 **SMOKING ROBOT**
2003 | 9½ x 4½ x 4¾ inches (24 x 11.5 x 12 cm)
A4 paper; template
Photo by Natsuyuki Kishimoto

accompanied their child to my workshop, get involved in cutting and pasting. They bring their finished models home as a treasure. That's when I think I've really accomplished something. **HOW HAS YOUR TECHNIQUE DEVELOPED?** There are countless ways to unfold a three-dimensional form to a two-dimensional plan. I needed to try many patterns to find the best way when I started paper craft. Now it's getting easier to reproduce a certain form efficiently and make the

MAKE CITY: LONDON ▶

2008 | Each: 2 x 2 x 2 inches (5 x 5 x 5 cm) each
Postcard-size paper; template
Photo by Natsuyuki Kishimoto

SEE
NO
EVIL

HEAR
NO
EVIL

SPEAK
NO
EVIL

THE GOLDEN RULE

2008 | 7 x 11 x 3¼ inches (18 x 28 x 8.5 cm)
Letter-size paper; template
Photo by Natsuyuki Kishimoto

moving images look charming. **HOW HAS YOUR SUBJECT MATTER EVOLVED?** At first, I was interested in detailed constructions as paper sculpture and 3D illustration. I sometimes made presents of small works for my friends. One day I decided to give them some cutting materials with instructions for assembly in place of a completed work. Realizing that they enjoyed the process

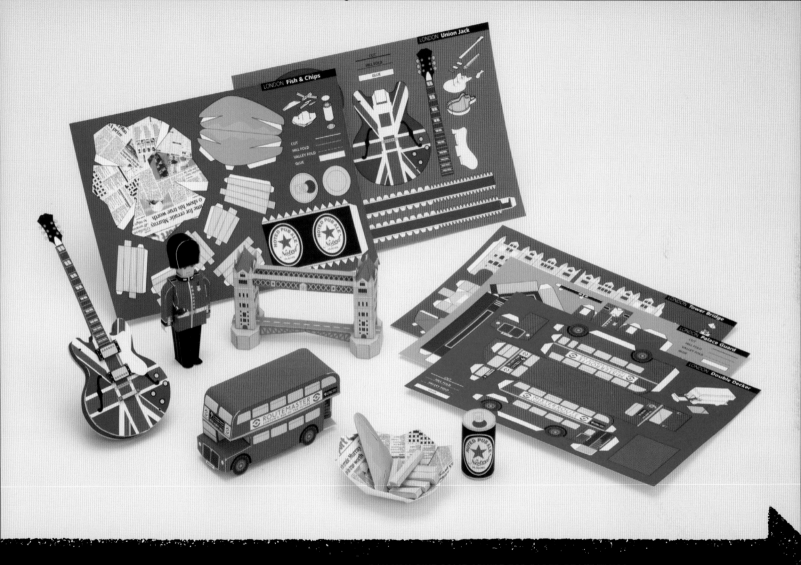

of construction, I decided this style was a better fit for me. **CAN YOU GIVE SOME ADVICE FOR PAPER CRAFT FANS?** Please, *please* read the instructions carefully before losing your temper.

SAELEE OH
UNITED STATES

"I love the flatness and delicateness of paper, the shadows it casts, and the fragility of the material."

◀ A SLIVER AND A SLICE
2010 | 60 x 40 inches (152.4 x 101.6 cm)
Paper
Photo by artist

DESCRIBE YOUR WORK. Dreamy flora and fauna. Magical wonderment. Silhouettes of daydreams and secret whispers. **EARLY INFLUENCES?** Storybooks, making mud pies and sandcastles. Being bored in school and doodling on my canvas three-ring binder while listening to lectures about mammals and insects, ancient civilizations, and geometry. **WHAT RESPONSES DO YOU GET TO YOUR WORK?** Usually pleasant and gentled-hearted people connect to my work. My mom is both my critic and biggest collector. She hangs everything in her house. It's like a Saelee Oh retrospective museum, and she doesn't complain if I take back a piece to sell to a collector. She thinks that means I'll give her more

WE NEED MORE ALPHABET LETTERS
2009 | 16 x 11 inches (40.6 x 27.9 cm)
Paper, acrylic, graphite
Photos by artist

NAPTIME IN THE FOREST ▶
2005 | 15 x 11 inches (38.1 x 27.9 cm)
Paper, dried flowers
Photo by artist

work to fill the walls. **WALK ME THROUGH A DAY IN YOUR STUDIO.** When I make work, I start by cleaning my entire space. I like to start with a very organized workspace to help clear my mind. Sometimes I play music, sometimes I don't. Sometimes I play the same song over and over again. I like to have a stash of food by me and work late into the night. I'm easily distracted and multitask constantly. It's only when I'm tired that I can sit down for longer periods of

time. If I get too tired, I get very sad, then go to bed and start all over again. **HOW HAS YOUR SUBJECT MATTER EVOLVED?** It's very, very subtle, but I think I started making more melancholy imagery. **WHAT INSPIRES YOU THESE DAYS?** I like going to random open houses to see people's private spaces. I like seeing people's collections of objects and art on the wall in the context of a cozy, intimate space rather than in a gallery with a price list. I also love all plants, trees, woods

◀| **INFINITE PATH**
2010 | 60 x 40 inches (152.4 x 101.6 cm)
Paper
Photo by artist

vines, and flowers, even though I don't like taking care of them, and I only have one plant. **HOW HAS YOUR TECHNIQUE DEVELOPED?**
I learned the hard way, after many blisters on my fingers, that I should switch to using thinner paper, and this let me make
more detailed, delicate cuts. Discovering the Japanese screw punch made making eyes for my characters a whole lot easier.

SHIPWRECK ISLAND

2009 | 36 x 48 inches (91.4 x 121.9 cm)
Paper and house paint
Photo by artist

I still question why I make my large paper cutouts because they're really frustrating to transport and mount onto the background, but I'm working towards the direction of bigger and more complex. Sometimes I combine painting with my cutouts and sometimes I don't.

INGRID SILIAKUS
THE NETHERLANDS

"Paper has a mind of its own and asks for cooperation rather than manipulation."

◀ **REFLECTION ON SAGRADA FAMILIA (WHITE VERSION)**

2008 | 23¾ x 11¾ x 11¾ inches
(60 x 30 x 30 cm)
Paper; integrated tabs
Photos by artist

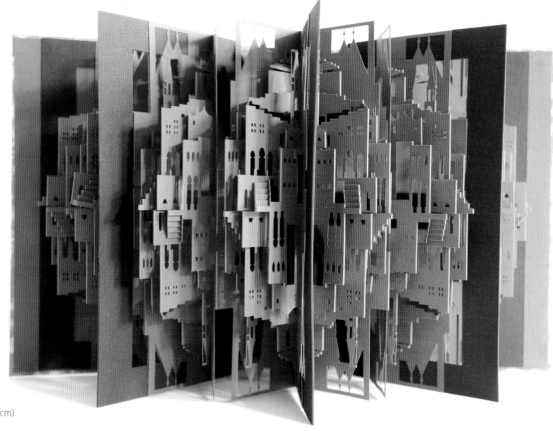

REFLEJAR

2008 | 8½ x 6¼ x 6¼ inches (22 x 16 x 16 cm)
Paper, cardboard folder
Photo by artist

DESCRIBE YOUR WORK. Paper architecture is the art of creating an object out of a single piece of paper. Before a sculpture can be created, a paper-architecture design has to be made. This process can take up to several weeks, to months. It is not uncommon to end up with 30 and sometimes upwards of 50 separate designs before I'm satisfied with the final design. Drawing paper architecture designs is like building: first one layer is drawn with a single shape and then layer after layer is added, adjusted, and altered. After the design stage, a paper-architecture artwork is created by a combination of detailed cutting and folding. **EARLY INFLUENCES?** My work has mainly been

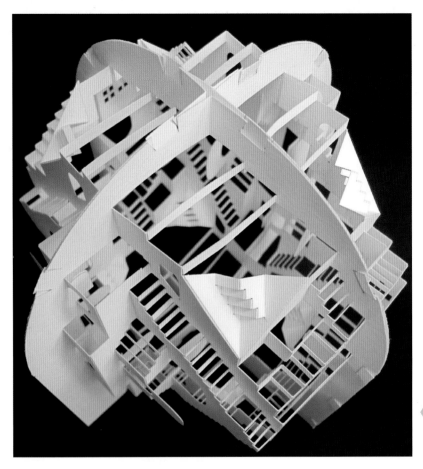

RONDDING HISTAIR
2010 | 5½ x 5½ x 4¾ inches (14 x 12 x 12 cm)
Rives Artist paper; cut, folded, integrated tabs and slits
Photo by artist

influenced by Japanese professor Masahiro Chatani, the originator of paper architecture, though he called it "origamic architecture." **HOW HAS YOUR TECHNIQUE DEVELOPED?** It has developed in the sense that the pieces are getting more intricate. I started out with simple buildings that got more complicated over time. The next step was making abstract pieces, originally inspired by the oeuvre of M.C. Escher. For the exhibition at the Museum Rijswijk during the international Holland Paper Biennial 2006, I made my first (round) sculpture that consisted of four sides ("innerrings") which also had an inside design. These days I am making more designs with multiple buildings

COVER WALLPAPER ▶
2009 | 8¼ x 12 x 8¼ inches (21 x 30 x 21 cm)
Paper; cut
Photo by artist

and/or multiple abstract objects included. **WHAT RESPONSES DO YOU GET TO YOUR WORK?** People feel attracted to it for various reasons. One of the things I hear is that my work has a kind of serenity. I also hear people in disbelief that my pieces can be created out of a single piece of paper by means of just cutting and folding. In the Western world paper architecture is not common, so a lot of people find it fascinating and intriguing. **WHAT INSPIRES YOU THESE DAYS?** The work of architects all over the world is inspiring.

"I find myself discovering new shapes, textures, and techniques the more I play around with paper."

SHANGHAI LADY
2005 | 8 x 10 x 1 inches (20.3 x 25.4 x 2.5 cm)
Paper, paint, glue
Photo by Scott Groller

KALI
2004 | 16 x 20 x 1 inches (40.6 x 50.8 x 2.5 cm)
Paper, paint, glue
Photo by Scott Groller

DESCRIBE YOUR WORK. My shapes are very graphic, and I work to give my pieces dimension by manipulating and layering paper. I'm very inspired by the design aesthetic of the 1950s and 60s. **EARLY INFLUENCES?** My father was a big influence on me pursuing visual arts. He is a veteran in the animation industry and a watercolorist. **HOW DID YOU START WORKING IN PAPER?** I took a design and color course at the Chouinard Foundation. My teacher, Leo Monahan, is a prolific paper sculptor, and his work inspired me to play with the medium. **WHAT RESPONSES DO YOU GET TO YOUR WORK?** I think people are very intrigued by paper art. People have told me that they appreciate the detail, texture, and dimension.

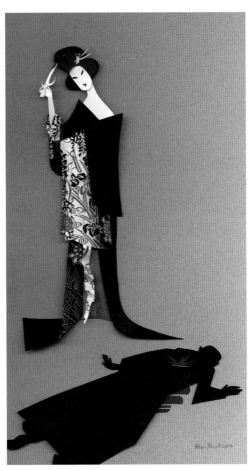

KUNOICHI—FEMALE NINJA
2007 | 10 x 20 x 1 inches (25.4 x 50.8 x 2.5 cm)
Paper, paint, glue
Photos by Scott Groller

IKEBANA
2006 | 31 x 18 x 3 inches (78.7 x 45.7 x 7.6 cm)
Paper, paint, glue
Photo by Scott Groller

that I add to my work. **HOW HAS YOUR SUBJECT MATTER EVOLVED?** When I first started creating paper sculptures, I was inspired by vintage fashion, animals, and world cultures. In the future I look forward to creating work that has interesting environments and more dynamic composition. **WHAT DO YOU LOVE ABOUT WORKING WITH PAPER?** I like how versatile it is and I love how light reacts to paper surfaces. Paper is such a great medium because it is so cheap, lightweight, and malleable. It is also easy to experiment with various compositions until I hit on one that I like. **WHAT INSPIRES YOU THESE DAYS?** World cultures, fashion, and mid-century modern design. **OTHER ARTISTS THAT INSPIRE YOU?** My husband, Shannon

AFRICAN BUTTERFLY
2008 | 10 x 20 x 1 inches (25.4 x 50.8 x 2.5 cm)
Paper, paint, glue
Photo by artist

Tindle, is a great artist, and he exposed me to artists such as Charley Harper, Eyvind Earle, and Mary Blair. I also love the work of Gruau, Erté, Tadahiro Uesugi, and Sanna Annukka. I am also very inspired by artists that are my friends in the animation industry, such as Kevin Dart, Chris Turnham, Dan Krall, Nicolas Marlet, Sanjay Patel, Lou

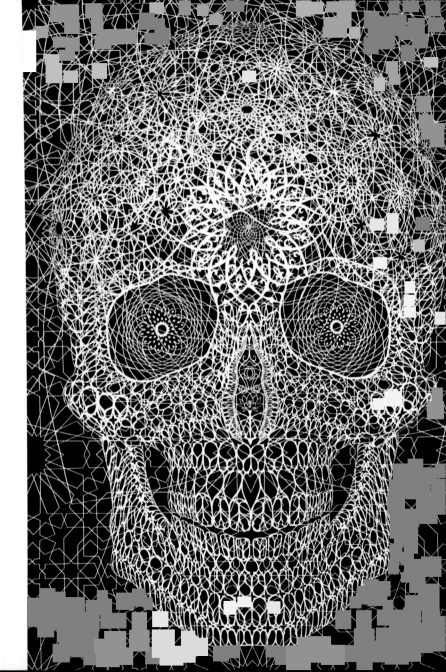

HUNTER STABLER

UNITED STATES

"It is my aim to create magical and spatially complex work that is in conversation with ancient, canonical, modernist, and contemporary ideas of spatiality in art making."

HARE CHRISTMAS MAHARISHI

2008 | 44 x 30 inches (111.8 x 76.2 cm)
Ink, graphite, paper
Photos by artist

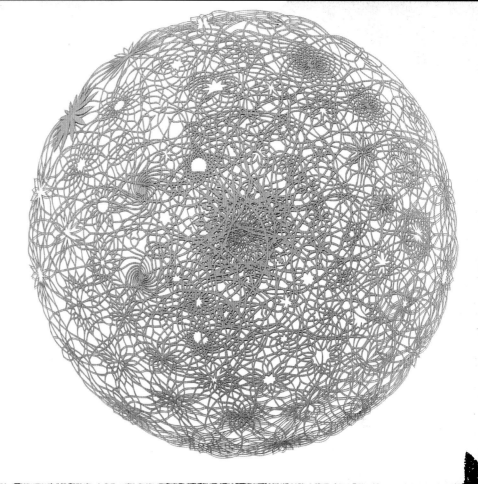

ORACULAR SEPHIROTIC HELIOSPECTRASCOPIGRAM ⏵

2008 | 40 x 40 inches (101.6 x 101.6 cm)
Ink, graphite, hand-cut paper, Plexiglas
Photo by artist

Q&A

DESCRIBE YOUR WORK. My work deals with architecture, patterning, and symbols of mystical and esoteric origins. I use multicultural religious-based patterns and cymatic patterns to construct images of mythical creatures, subtle invisible phenomena, theoretical shapes of the universe, and microcosmic vibratory events. The formal aspects of my work involve a play between the illusion of space, actual physical space, and the two-dimensionality of the paper. Perspectival patterning creates the illusion of form. Flat patterning defines the surface of the picture plane, and a

physical cast shadow shows the actual space and thinness of the paper. **HOW DID YOU END UP WORKING WITH PAPER?** I started working with paper in undergraduate school as a simple analogue way to work with quadrant symmetry, by folding the paper twice and cutting it. It was a throwback to the paper snowflake that we all made in elementary school. **HOW HAS YOUR TECHNIQUE DEVELOPED?** I pencil and ink my work now before I cut it. I cut with a regular X-Acto

knife. Basically, my technique developed from doing a very similar but increasingly complex task for the past 10 years. **WALK ME THROUGH A DAY IN YOUR STUDIO.** I basically just sit at a modified architect's drafting table all day and either draw or cut on a sheet of paper while listening to some heavy music. **HOW HAS YOUR SUBJECT MATTER EVOLVED?** My subject matter has kind of revolved around similar interests for a long time. I have learned a lot more about

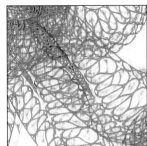

◀◀ **SAINT VITUS ARCHITEUTHIS MANALISHI WITH THE SEVEN TENTACLE CROWN**
2008 | 44 x 44 inches (111.8 x 111.8 cm)
Ink, graphite, hand-cut paper, color-aid, Plexiglas
Photos by artist

esoterism and magical sigils and pan-cultural mysticism, which has made my subject matter more specific in some cases. **WHAT INSPIRES YOU THESE DAYS?** Cuttlefish, nebulas, and most things I see on NOVA. **WHAT ARTISTS INSPIRE YOU?** So many: Charles Ray, Wim Delvoye, Are Mokkelbost, Thomas Woodruff, and too many to name here. **WHAT DO YOU LOVE ABOUT WORKING WITH PAPER?** I really love the repetitive activity of cutting small pieces out of a large sheet of paper. It's

◀ **SATOR SQUARE**
2009 | 12 x 12 inches (30.5 x 30.5 cm)
Ink, graphite, hand-cut paper, color-aid, Plexiglas
Photo by artist

similar, I imagine, to the satisfaction of weaving but combined with the pleasure of peeling paint with your fingernail. **EARLY INFLUENCES?** Gregory Green, Andy Kaufman, John and James Whitney, Mati Klarwein, Bridget Riley, Richard Anuszkiewicz, Middle Eastern rugs, Islamic tile, cathedral architecture, Chinese lattices, Hindu and Buddhist sculpture, and anything else imbued with the ancient pattern-oriented intricacy of psychedelic froth

"If I want to erase, I just use an X-Acto knife."

EXPORT THE OUTPUT

2008 | 48 x 96 x 6 inches (121.9 x 243.8 x 15.2 cm)
Pine, masonite, chipboard, tape, glue, acrylic sealer
Photo by Mark Moore Gallery

BOOM-BOOM
2009 | 36 x 16 x 10 inches (91.4 x 40.6 x 25.4 cm)
Chipboard, cardboard, tape, glue, acrylic sealer
Photo by Davidson Contemporary

Q&A

DESCRIBE YOUR WORK. Focused and fun. **EARLY INFLUENCES?** My parents, local artists in my hometown, all the guys at *Mad Magazine*, George Lucas, Hanna-Barbera, Disney, and *Looney Tunes*. **HOW DID YOU END UP WORKING WITH PAPER?** I made stuff out of paper cardboard when I was a kid but it wasn't until I was asked to do a big installation for a show—I had no money and the organizers had no money, so I built the piece out of cardboard. **WHAT RESPONSES DO YOU GET TO YOUR WORK?** I hear "Wow, crazy man, awesome," and, "You must have a lot of time on your hands." **HOW HAS YOUR TECHNIQUE DEVELOPED?** Time, patience, experimentation, and looking at other people's work. **WHAT WOULD BE YOUR**

DREAM CARDBOARD STRUCTURE? It would be pretty insane to build a super high-tech, state of the art, mega-telescope with all the possible options, like the fancy new one they have at Griffith Observatory. I would want real lenses in it if I were going to do it. I'd like the viewer to at least see something through the eyepiece when looking in. Maybe I could do an animation that would run inside and take the viewer on a journey through our universe—or maybe it would just look at a brick wall. **WHAT DO YOU LOVE ABOUT WORKING WITH PAPER?** The immediacy. I love the way it reacts much like drawing for me. You see a shape, and, in a matter of minutes, you can be sitting next to that very shape you saw in your head. **HOW HAS YOUR SUBJECT MATTER EVOLVED?** I don't feel I have a particular subject matter. Lately, I want to build

anything that seems complicated. It becomes about the challenge of interpreting the objects. However, the detail, quality, and craft of the objects I build has evolved. I can't believe I even let some of the early stuff out in public, now that I have been working with this material for a few years. There are still so many more places to take this medium. **WHAT INSPIRES YOU THESE DAYS?** Other artists, new music, Google images, stories I hear from friends, my girlfriend, getting out and traveling. A recent trip to Thailand has been an endless source of inspiration lately. **OTHER ARTISTS THAT INSPIRE YOU?** Honestly, anyone who uses their hands to make stuff is an inspiration. A few of my absolute favorites include Travis Millard, Tom Sachs, H.C. Westermann, Klai Brown, and Pal Wright.

DAN McPHARLIN

AUSTRALIA

"Working with paper or cardboard doesn't require expensive tools or a sophisticated studio. I find the process is relatively quick from idea to finished product."

UNTITLED

2007 | 3¼ x 4 x 2 inches (8 x 10 x 5 cm)
Framing matt boards, paper, cord, glue, paint
Photo by artist

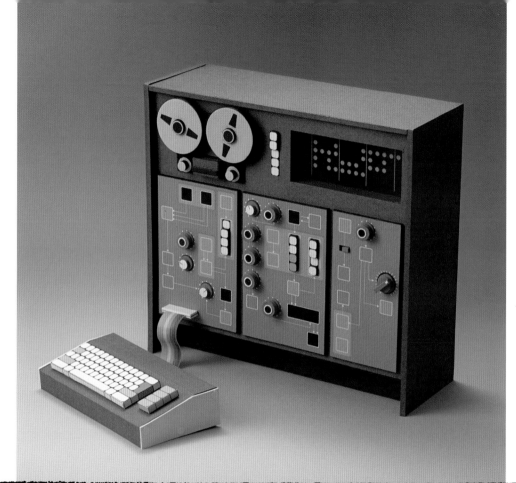

◀ UNTITLED
2007 | 6¼ x 6¼ x 2 inches (16 x 16 x 5 cm)
Framing matt boards, paper, plastic sheeting, glue, paint
Photos by artist

DESCRIBE YOUR WORK. The cardboard models I made between 2006 and 2009 were my attempt to create a series of objects that paid tribute to the first wave of synthesizers and analogue recording equipment from a time when electronic music was about experimentation and discovery, and before the synthesizer was thought of as simply another keyboard instrument. **EARLY INFLUENCES?** I grew up cherishing certain objects—particularly records and books, things that were beautifully designed or had artwork you could get lost in for hours. I have always loved modernist design and architecture, science fiction, and electronic music. **HOW DID YOU END UP WORKING WITH PAPER?** We had a framing

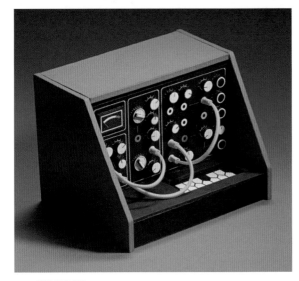

 UNTITLED

2007 | 3½ x 4 x 2 inches (9 x 10 x 5 cm)
Framing matt boards, paper, rubber bands, glue, paint
Photo by artist

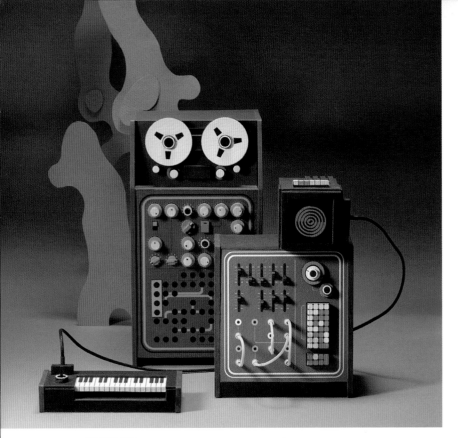

 UNTITLED

2008 | 7 x 7 x 7 inches (18 x 18 x 18 cm)
Framing matt boards, paper, rubber bands, plastic sheeting, glue, paint
Photo by artist

business in the family, and I noticed the matt board offcuts were going to waste, so I stepped in and started building small sculptures with them. When I felt I'd honed my craft, I focused on building the Analogue Miniatures. **WHAT RESPONSES DO YOU GET TO YOUR WORK?** Responses are generally very positive, although some people assume I have some kind of obsessive-compulsive disorder. Well, maybe they're right! **HOW HAS YOUR SUBJECT MATTER EVOLVED?** Gosh, it hasn't really! I'm trapped in the past. **WHAT DO YOU LOVE ABOUT WORKING WITH PAPER?** Its versatility. It has a 2D surface,

▌ **UNTITLED**
2007 | 3¼ x 3¼ x 5 inches (8 x 13 x 13 cm)
Framing matt boards, paper, glue, paint
Photo by artist

but it can also be sculptural. Cardboard can be made into very rigid shapes that are suitable for furniture or even buildings. In the 1960s, architect Frank Gehry was pioneering the use of cardboard to make lightweight, inexpensive furniture, but then plastic took on that role. Now I think there is a resurgence of interest with many young artists rediscovering the medium.

"I aim to create an experience of wonder we were all familiar with during childhood."

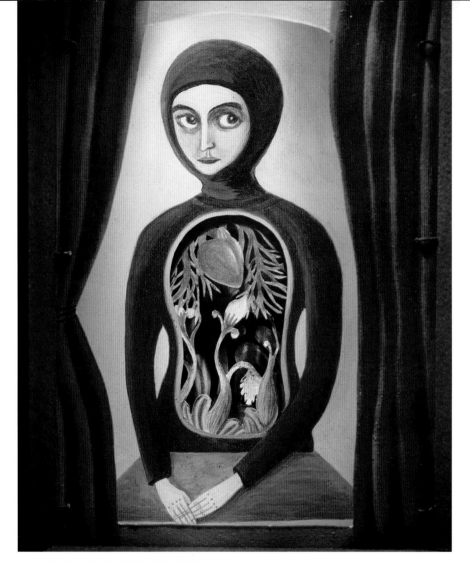

SELF PORTRAIT WITH INSIDE VIEW
2008 | 5 x 7 x 6 inches (12.7 x 17.8 x 15.2 cm)
Multi-layered collapsible tunnel book, hand-cut paper, thread, acrylic paint, mixed media
Photo by Péter Hapák

◀ INSIDE THE HEART
2009 | 5 x 7 x 6 inches (12.7 x 17.8 x 15.2 cm)
Multi-layered collapsible tunnel book, hand-cut
paper, thread, acrylic paint, mixed media
Photos by Péter Hapák

Q&A

DESCRIBE YOUR WORK. My work is personal, representational, narrative, and it ranges across media. I make drawings; small, densely worked up one-of-a-kind artist's books; intricate, multi-layered paper cutouts; embroidery; sculpture; installation; animation and large-scale murals. Sometimes I use traditional craft media to explore controversial subject matter. **EARLY INFLUENCES?** Nadia Comaneci and Yuri Gagarin. **HOW HAS YOUR SUBJECT MATTER EVOLVED?** My subject matter is my lived experience; it's something that has always been there, always available for exploration. **WHAT WAS**

IT LIKE GROWING UP IN AN URBAN HOUSING DEVELOPMENT IN COMMUNIST ROMANIA? We hiked almost every Sunday, vacationed in the mountains in Transylvania and at the Black Sea every summer. I took art and piano lessons; biked and swam during the summer, skated and skied during the winter. I was enrolled in various sports from table tennis to gymnastics, fencing, orienteering, karate and judo—these things were either free or quite affordable. We roamed free in

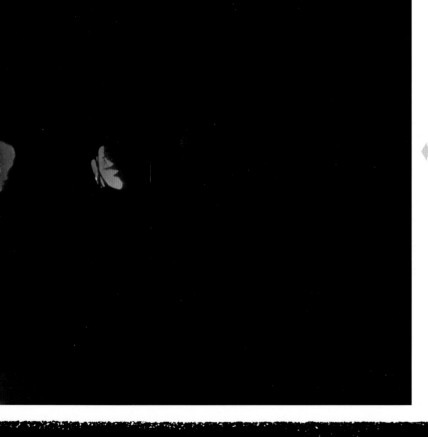

SOMETIMES IN MY DREAMS I FLY

2010 | 540 x 144 x 240 inches (1371.6 x 365.8 x 609.6 cm)
Tunnel book installation, Rice Gallery, Houston, Texas
Hand-cut gator board, laser cut paper, wire, lights, color gels, acrylic paint, vinyl cutouts, glass
Photo by Nash Baker

the city and the neighboring woods with our friends. Our meals were made from scratch, seasonally from produce our mothers bought at the farmers market. I held student season passes to the theater, symphony, and opera. When I was thirteen, my friends and I wrote serialized novels with girls like us as protagonists. We'd discuss the latest installment, which usually ended on a cliffhanger, as a group, and suggested ideas for the next one. I found the

SOMETIMES IN MY DREAMS I FLY (DETAILS)
Photos by Nash Baker

clothes sold in the stores uninspiring, so I created my own fashion by sewing from scratch or altering and custom-izing vintage clothes in my mother's and grandmother's closets. There was no pressure that I should study something practical or chose a career that would help me make money since there was no money to be made. **HOW DID YOU END UP WORKING WITH PAPER?** I began by working with paper and never stopped. **HOW DO YOU SUSTAIN YOUR**

FOCUS WHEN YOU WORK? For me it took practice to be able to sit and focus for long stretches of time. Sometimes it comes quite easily. Other times I listen to radio or TED talks, TV shows, or documentaries streamed through headphones from my laptop as I work. If I engage the verbal part of my mind with an absorbing narrative it doesn't nag me to get up and do something that makes more sense instead of finding my way through a visual art project. **OTHER ARTISTS THAT INSPIRE YOU?** Janet Cardiff, Tara Donovan, and Harmony Korine.

CHARLES CLARY

UNITED STATES

"There is something so freeing about using an extremely traditional material, something every artist commonly uses to draw upon, and transforming it into sprawling, large-scale installations."

FERMATIC WILDERNESS

2008 | 72 x 72 x 10 inches (182.9 x 182.9 x 25.4 cm)
Acrylic and hand-cut paper on panel
Photo by Charles Clary

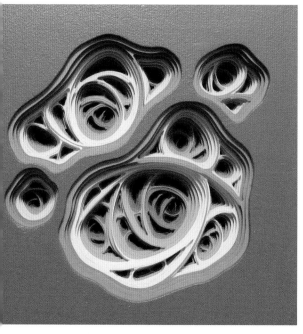

MICROBIAL DIDDLATION MOVEMENT #8

2010 | 10 x 10 x 3 inches (25.4 x 25.4 x 7.6 cm)
Acrylic and hand-cut paper on panel
Photos by Charles Clary

Q&A

DESCRIBE YOUR WORK. I use paper to create a world of fiction that challenges the viewer to suspend disbelief and venture into my fabricated reality. By layering paper I am able to build intriguing land formations that mimic viral colonies and concentric sound waves. **EARLY INFLUENCES?** A lot of things inspire me, including electron microscope images of viruses, microscopic life, mold, fungus, spores, topographic maps, aerial photography, cave systems, and artists such as Kara Walker, Daniel Zeller, Jane South, Noriko Ambe, Jen Stark, Damon Soule, Jeff Soto, and Aaron Noble. **HOW DID YOU END UP WORKING WITH PAPER?** I received a workspace in New York for a semester during grad school

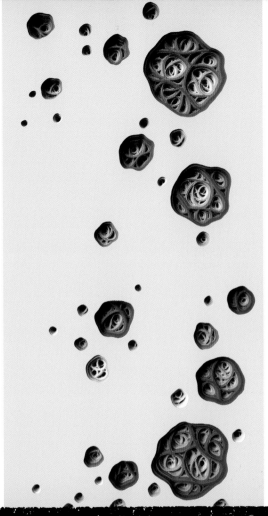

TRIPLE RADIMACUE INFESTATION
2008 | 96 x 480 x 10 inches (243 x 1219.2 x 25.4 cm)
Acrylic, and hand-cut paper on panel
Photo by Charles Clary

FERMATIC PANDEMIC MOVEMENT #1
2009 | 72 x 36 x 4 inches (182.9 x 91.4 x 10.2 cm)
Acrylic and hand cut paper on panel
Photos by Charles Clary

and had limited access to woodshop tools. I had all these ideas about free-flowing forms meandering across a wall space, but couldn't make them out of anything that needed to be cut with heavy-duty equipment. I was walking through the lower east side when I came across an interesting paper/scrapbook store and decided to go in. There, I found a particular type of card stock that was semi-rigid and came in a multitude of colors. Out of necessity I grabbed a stack, went back to the studio, and I haven't looked back since. **HOW HAS YOUR SUBJECT MATTER EVOLVED?**

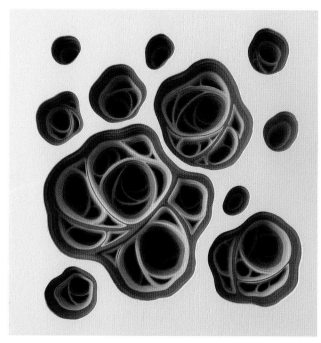

FLAMUNGLE GESTATION
2010 | 12 x 12 x 4 inches (30.5 x 30.5 x 10.2 cm)
Acrylic and hand-cut paper on panel
Photo by Charles Clary

DOUBLE DIDDLE EVISCERATION
2009 | 72 x 216 x 10 inches (182.9 x 548.6 x 25.4 cm)
Acrylic and hand-cut paper on panel
Photo by Charles Clary

My work used to be solely based on the idea of music and how it can have this viral-like affect on humanity. For a time I felt like a mad scientist creating this fictitious reality in a lab, under scrutiny. It was very Frankensteinish. But as the work has grown, it has encompassed so much more. I still relate it to music and this idea of things going viral, but it also embraces the idea of pandemics and bioengineered organisms. We use the term "viral" in many different contexts and it's interesting for me to explore this idea in a playful, inviting way.

MIA PEARLMAN

UNITED STATES

"I'm always looking for a way to invite chance into my process and you never know quite how paper will behave."

GYRE

2008 | Site-specific installation at the Islip Art Museum, Islip, New York
84 x 132 x 156 inches (213.4 x 335.3 x 396.2 cm)
Paper, India ink, tacks, paper clips
Photo by Gene Bahng

UPDRAFT

2008 | Site-specific installation at Mixed Greens, New York
96 x 144 x 78 inches (243.8 x 365.8 x 198.1 cm)
Paper, India ink, tacks, paper clips
Photo by Jason Mandella

DESCRIBE YOUR WORK. I make site-specific cut paper installations, ephemeral drawings in both two and three dimensions that blur the line between actual, illusionistic, and imagined space. Extremely sculptural and often glowing with natural or artificial light, these imaginary weather systems appear frozen in an ambiguous moment, bursting through or hovering within a room. **HOW DO YOU BEGIN?** My process is very intuitive, based on spontaneous decisions in the moment. I begin by making loose line drawings in India ink on large rolls of paper. Then I cut out selected areas between the lines to make a new drawing in positive and negative space on the reverse. Thirty to eighty of

MAELSTROM

2008 | Smack Mellon, Brooklyn, New York
Diameter: 144 inches (365.8 cm)
Steel, aluminum, paper, India ink, monofilament, wire
Photo by Jason Mandella

MAELSTROM (VIEW FROM UNDERNEATH)

2008 | Smack Mellon, Brooklyn, New York
Diameter: 144 inches (365.8 cm)
Steel, aluminum, paper, India ink, monofilament, wire
Photo by Jason Mandella

these cut paper pieces form the final installation, which I create on site by trial and error, a two to three day dance with chance and control. Existing only for the length of an exhibition, this weightless world totters on the brink of being and not being, continually in flux. It is my meditation on creation, destruction, and the transient nature of reality. **HOW DID YOU END UP WORKING WITH PAPER?** I've always drawn, and made works on paper. Even the thought of stretched canvas gives me the willies. The installations happened very suddenly without much warning. Originally, I had an

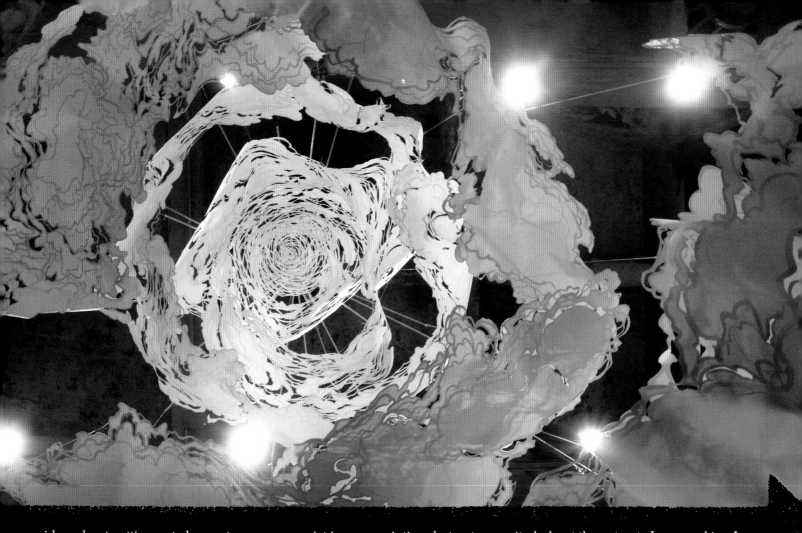

idea about cutting out shapes to use as a resist in monoprinting, but got so excited about the cut outs I was making I bagged the prints and started making images from layers of cut paper, kind of like collages but not glued down—it was very transitional work. That summer my husband and I rented a house and studio in Woodstock, New York, for a month. When I got there I pinned up these "collages" on the studio walls. Well, I guess I didn't do a very good job because when I walked downstairs the next morning they had come loose in areas and bent into the space of the

INRUSH
2009 | Site-specific installation at the Museum of Arts and Design, New York
192 x 60 x 48 inches (487.7 x 152.4 x 121.9 cm)
Paper, India ink, tacks, paper clips
Photos by Jason Mandella

room. And I thought, "Wow, that is really interesting." Within a week I had completed my first cut paper installation, WHORL, and a week later my second, TORNADO. **WHAT RESPONSES DO YOU GET TO YOUR WORK?** There is always some-one who asks me, "What is it? What is it made of?" And when I reply, "Paper," they confusedly ask, "How is it held together? Glue?" The minute I say "paper clips and tacks" it's like a light bulb goes off—everyone uses paper and

INFLUX ▶

2008 | Site-specific installation at Roebling Hall Gallery, New York
Dimensions variable
Paper, India ink, tacks, paper clips
Photo by Jason Mandella

paper clips and tacks. In that moment they realize that a very mundane and familiar material has been transformed into something quite surprising. **HOW HAS YOUR TECHNIQUE DEVELOPED?** My work is so intuitive, it requires a certain fearlessness to make—a faith in myself and my process that I didn't have as a younger artist.

HELEN MUSSELWHITE

UNITED KINGDOM

"My work has a distinctive handcrafted quality that pays respect to all forms of mid-century design, folk and ethnic art."

WHITE RABBIT HEDGEROW ⬤

2010 | 7½ x 14 x 1½ inches (19 x 36 x 4 cm)
Paper sculpture
Photo by artist

◀ HILLTOP HOUSE GLASS DOME

2010 | 12 x 5½ inches (30 x 14 cm)
Paper sculpture
Photos by artist

DESCRIBE YOUR WORK. My work is constructed from layers of colored, patterned, and textured paper. The subject matter is mostly the countryside, and flora and fauna, and I have a love for little cottages too! It's very detailed and stylized, and captures a moment or a perfect scene forever. **EARLY INFLUENCES?** Influences include mid-century modern designers and illustrators, Indian miniature paintings, Japanese decorative art, Victorian taxidermy, French marriage globes, and folk art. **HOW DID YOU END UP WORKING WITH PAPER?** I've always loved a clean, new sheet of paper (at school one of my favorite things was a brand new exercise book); it has so many possibilities. It's clean, crisp

NIBBLES WOOD ◗
2010 | 31½ x 39 x 28 inches (80 x 100 x 70 cm)
Layered paper photography set
Photo by artist

◖ **SUMMER OWL TREE**
2009 | 10 x 10 x 10 inches (25 x 25 x 25 cm)
Multi-layered paper sculpture
Photo by artist

and waiting to be transformed. **WHAT RESPONSES DO YOU GET TO YOUR WORK?** Lots of people say it reminds them of fairy tales and children's storybooks. They also notice the detail and comment on the time and patience it must take. I've heard people say they would like to climb into it, which is fantastic, as that's exactly what I'd like to do! **HOW HAS YOUR TECHNIQUE DEVELOPED?** Since I started paper cutting four years ago I've become more and more aware of the execution of each piece. The detail is very important. I've also started using glass domes so the viewer can walk around

a piece, look through it, and see it "in the round." It also means I can add more detail. **OTHER ARTISTS THAT INSPIRE YOU?** I like Picasso for his genius, his self belief and prolificacy. Andy Warhol too, particularly his commercial artwork of the 1950s. There are also many, mostly American illustrators of the 1950s and 60s that I've discovered through the Internet. **WHAT DO YOU LOVE ABOUT WORKING WITH PAPER?** I love that I can cut, fold, score, and curl a piece of flat paper into whatever I desire. It's immediate and if it goes wrong or I change my mind I can recycle and start again.

BEAUTIES WOODLAND COTTAGE
2010 | 20 x 20 x 20 inches (50 x 50 x 50 cm)
Multi-layered paper sculpture
Photo by artist

BEAUTIES BUTTERFLY
2009 | 20 x 20 x 20 inches (50 x 50 x 50 cm)
Multi-layered paper sculpture
Photo by artist

"Paper is not perma-
nent, but that is what
makes paper work
beautiful."

THREE
2008 | 7 x 2¼ x 2¼ linches (18 x 6 x 6 cm)
Paper
Photo by artist

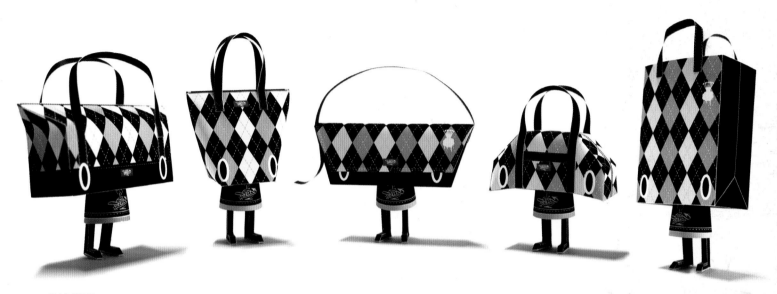

 **BAGGIES**
2010 | Each: 4 x 4 x 2 inches (10 x 10 x 5 cm)
Paper
Photo by artist

DESCRIBE YOUR WORK. I make paper toys. **EARLY INFLUENCES?** Hip-hop culture and graffiti art. I didn't go to school to study art; I taught myself. I traveled to many countries to check out street graffiti and became absorbed in the hip-hop culture. **HOW DID YOU END UP WORKING WITH PAPER?** Paper is the most familiar material for me. **WALK ME THROUGH A DAY IN YOUR STUDIO.** I don't have a studio. In other words, I don't need a studio: I just need scissors and glue. **WHAT INSPIRES YOU THESE DAYS?** Hip-hop music. When I'm thinking of a new idea, I always listen to it at mega volume. Break beats and rhymes bring fresh inspiration to me. **OTHER ARTISTS THAT INSPIRE YOU?** Andy Warhol, Banksy, and Michael Lau.

T-BOY

2009 | Each: 6 x 3¼ x 2 inches (15 x 8 x 5 cm)
Paper and vinyl
Photo by artist

WHAT DO YOU LOVE ABOUT WORKING WITH PAPER? Paper provides a way for me to express myself. **HOW DID YOU START CREATING PAPER TOYS?** To draw graffiti on a street wall is illegal, so I was looking for an alternative canvas. My solution was to create paper toys. I designed a white paper toy as my graffiti canvas—it's the origin of my creations. When I was young I played with origami which ultimately helped me design paper toy templates. **WHAT IS THE BIGGEST CHALLENGE IN THE ART OF MAKING PAPER TOYS?** To collaborate with as many people as possible. Paper is a great medium because I can send a template via e-mail and people anywhere in the world can print it out and build it. If they draw something on

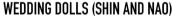 **WEDDING DOLLS (SHIN AND NAO)**
2010 | Each: 6 x 2 x 2 inches (15 x 5 x 5 cm)
Paper
Photo by artist

T-BOY
2010 | 6 x 3¼ x 2 inches (15 x 8 x 5 cm)
Paper
Photo by artist

the surface, the designed template can be returned to me much easier than other materials, like vinyl toys. **DESCRIBE A DAY IN YOUR LIFE.** Every day I receive e-mails from people all over the world. Some people ask me for my paper toy templates, some send me a designed template and photo they customized, and others ask me how to be a toy artist. I receive a lot of inspiration and feedback everyday. This is all I hoped for when I stared my art career. My dreams have come true. **OTHER ACHIEVEMENTS?** I support art education for kids. My paper toys are used in art curriculums in many schools, from elementary schools to university classes, in over 200 schools worldwide.

BOXY

2008 | Each: 3¼ x 4 x ¾ inches (8 x 10 x 2 cm)
Paper
Photo by artist

T-BOY AND HOOPHY

2010 | Each: 8 x 4 x 4 inches (20 x 10 x 10 cm)
Paper
Photo by artist

THE ARTISTS / INDEX

MATT HAWKINS (PAGE 96)

is a paper toy artist, illustrator, cartoonist, and incessant doodler living in Kansas City. He has shown his work in art galleries and exhibitions from Los Angeles to Amsterdam to Tokyo. Matt's paper toys and paper sculpture illustrations have been featured in many books and magazines. Hawkins is the author of *Urban Paper*, a book that features the world's best paper toy artists. (Artist photo on page 96 by Richard Daley.)

www.paperforest.com
www.custompapertoys.com

ROB IVES (PAGE 32)

began designing models made from cardboard after working for a decade as a teacher. Over the years, he has created many models and now works full time as a designer and paper engineer. He lives in Cumbria County in the United Kingdom with his wife, Pauline, and their two children, Martha and Elliot.

www.robives.com
www.flying-pig.co.uk

KIEL JOHNSON (PAGE 136)

started life in Kansas City, Kansas. After 25 years of adventures in and around the Midwest, Kiel decided to move to Los Angeles, where he founded Hyperbole Studios and began making stuff. At this pace, he hopes to be leaving LA in June 2024. For now, however, he can almost always be found working diligently in the studio.

www.kieljohnson.com

BOVEY LEE (PAGE 44)

is a Hong Kong-born, Pittsburgh-based artist. Her paper cutouts contemporize the fading Chinese folk art of paper cutting. Bovey's work has been exhibited internationally, including the Museum Bellerive (Switzerland); National Glass Centre (United Kingdom); Museum Rijswijk (The Netherlands); Brooklyn Museum of Art (New York); Museum of Fine Arts, Beijing (China); and Fukuoka Museum of Art (Japan). She is a recipient of many awards and has work in the permanent collections at Oxford University and the Hong Kong Museum of Art.

www.boveylee.com

NIKKI McCLURE (PAGE 78)

of Olympia, Washington, is known for her beautifully intricate paper cuts. Armed with an X-Acto knife, she cuts out her images from a single sheet of paper and creates a bold language that translates the complex poetry of motherhood, nature, and activism into a simple and endearing picture. She regularly produces her own posters, books, cards, T-shirts, and a yearly calendar. She is a self-taught artist who has been making papercuts since 1996.

www.nikkimcclure.com

JAYME McGOWAN (PAGE 38)

is a California-based artist and illustrator. She builds whimsical, three-dimensional environments with playful characters, all hand cut and intricately assembled. In addition to creating illustrations for a wide array of clients, Jayme regularly exhibits her original cut-paper works in the United States and abroad. She documents her unique form of papercraft with in-progress photos and notes about her process on her studio blog.

www.roadsideprojects.com

THE ARTISTS / INDEX

ROB RYAN (PAGE 26)

was born in Akrotiri, Cyprus. He studied Fine Art at Trent Polytechnic and the Royal College of Art, London, where he specialized in Printmaking. Since 2002, he has been working principally within the paper-cutting medium. Ryan has collaborated with Paul Smith, Liberty of London, Fortnum & Mason, and *Vogue*, and his work has been exhibited all over the world, including in the show, *Slash: Paper Under the Knife* at the Modern Art Museum, New York. He lives and works in London. (Artist photo on page 26 by Suzie Winsor.)

www.misterrob.co.uk

KEISUKE SAKA (PAGE 110)

is a paper engineer and graphic designer based in Japan. His mechanical paper toys are characterized by clear color, simple forms, and charming characters. His models, especially his *karakuri* (automata) series, have been released in several countries and many are available online for download.

www.zuko.to/kobo/

JARED ANDREW SCHORR (PAGE 90)

is an illustrator living in Southern California. He received his BFA in Illustration from the Art Center College of Design in Pasadena. Schorr's work has appeared in the *New York Times, Bust, GOOD, WIRED,* and *Poketo,* and can be seen on living room walls around the world.

www.jaredandrewschorr.com

INGRID SILAKUS (PAGE 122)

is a self-taught paper artist renowned for her work in paper architecture—an art form with its roots in Japan, best described as forming objects out of a single sheet of paper. Her work is characteristically complex with a high level of detail, and her designs are architectural, figurative, and abstract.

ingrid-siliakus.exto.org

MATTHEW SPORZYNSKI (PAGE 10)

was born in Ann Arbor, Michigan, and studied at Parsons School of Design in New York City. His work has appeared in *Town & Country, Vogue, Harper's Bazaar, GQ,* and *Real Simple,* and his corporate clients have included The Estée Lauder Companies, Tiffany & Co., The Museum of Modern Art, Christian Dior, Target, Macy's, and Polo Ralph Lauren.

HUNTER STABLER (PAGE 130)

lives and works in Philadelphia, Pennsylvania. He received his BFA from Maryland Institute College of Art in 2003, and his MFA from the University of Pennsylvania in 2006. His work has been widely shown across the United States, and overseas in Germany. Hunter's work has been published by *New Lights Press, First Look Magazine,* and *DIF* magazine.

www.hunterstabler.com

JEN STARK (PAGE 104)

was born in Miami, Florida, and attended New World School of the Arts High School. She went on to graduate with a BFA from Maryland Institute College of Art in 2005, majoring in Fibers with a minor in Animation. She has exhibited her works in various galleries as well as the Girls' Club Collection in Florida, the Museum of Art in Fort Lauderdale, and the Museum of Contemporary Art in Miami. She was a recipient of the prestigious South Florida Cultural Consortium's Visual and Media Artists Fellowship in 2008. Stark lives and works in Miami. (Artist photo on page 104 by Gwen Williams.)

www.jenstark.com

THE ARTISTS / INDEX

JILL SYLVIA (PAGE 100)

was born in Plymouth, Massachusetts, and lives in San Francisco, California. She holds an MFA from the San Francisco Art Institute and a BA from Bard College. Her work has been largely exhibited in San Francisco and the Bay Area, and in such cities as New York, Los Angeles, Minneapolis, Milwaukee, and Las Vegas. Sylvia has held solo exhibitions at Eleanor Harwood Gallery in San Francisco and Julian Page Fine Art in London. She looks forward to a forthcoming show at Magrorocca in Milan.

www.jillsylvia.com

SHIN TANAKA (PAGE 166)

was once a graffiti artist in search of an interesting canvas instead of a street wall. One day, he hit upon the idea to draw graffiti on a toy. He ended up making his own toy out of paper, drawing from the origami experiences of his youth. Today, Tanaka is well known for his paper toys, which exude a charming blend of street culture, pop art, graffiti, and street fashion. When he designs new work, he plays hip-hop music at mega volume, taking inspiration from the beats and flow. Tanaka lives in Japan.

www.shin.co.nr

MICHAEL VELLIQUETTE (PAGE 66)

has shown his work at DCKT Contemporary (New York), David Shelton Gallery (San Antonio), and the John Michael Kohler Art Center (Sheboygan). Museum exhibitions include *Slash: Paper Under the Knife* at the Museum of Art and Design (New York); and *Psychedelic* at the San Antonio Museum of Art. He is currently an Associate Faculty member in the Art Department at the University of Wisconsin–Madison.

www.velliquette.com

ANNIE VOUGHT (PAGE 22)

was raised in Santa Fe, New Mexico, and grew up surrounded by the arts. Her intricate work explores emotional artifacts, specifically in the form of the handwritten letter. In 1999, she co-directed The Budget Gallery, a roving art gallery in San Francisco, as well as the Boathouse Gallery. In 2009, she received her MFA from Mills College. Vought lives in Oakland, California, with her husband and large dog. Her work is exhibited far and wide.

www.annievought.com

ABOUT THE JUROR

Jaime Zollars paints pictures of imaginary people and far away places. She is an illustrator for children's books, magazines, newspapers, and ad campaigns. Her work has appeared in Taschen's *Illustration Now!*, *American Illustration*, *Communication Arts*, *3x3*, *Spectrum*, *Curvy*, *Design Taxi*, *XFuns*, and *DPI*, among other places. When she isn't painting for commercial clients or gallery walls, you'll find Jaime making mechanical paper toys, reading up on North Korea, or teaching talented young illustrators at the Maryland Institute College of Art.

ACKNOWLEDGMENTS

I'd like to thank the amazing contributors to the Paper Forest blog (www.paperforestblog.com) who have inspired me with their thoughtful content, helped me when I've become too busy to post much as I'd like, and introduced me to some of the wonderful artists in this book. Matt Hawkins, Falk Keuten, Shelley Noble, and Dan McPharlin, thanks for being a part of my obsession, and for sharing your knowledge on Paper Forest over the past several years. Thanks also to my *PUSH Paper* editor, Kathleen McCafferty, who allowed me to indulge in my love for these paper artists and share some of my favorites in this gorgeous volume.